Introduction

The sea has beautiful creatures, so many children like to draw them, But they don't know where and how to start.

This book will teach children and beginners how to draw sea animals step by step with a simple drawing method.

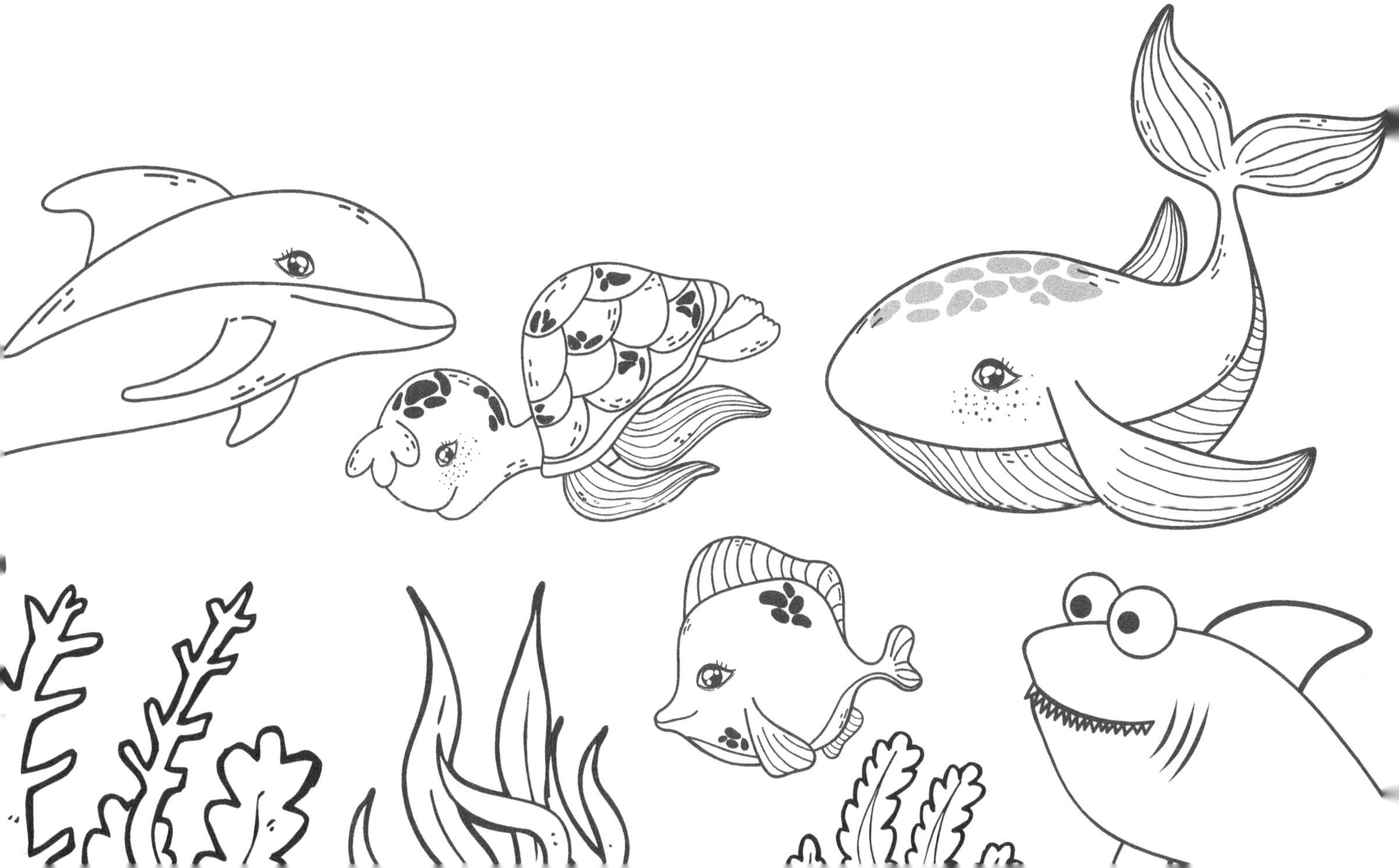

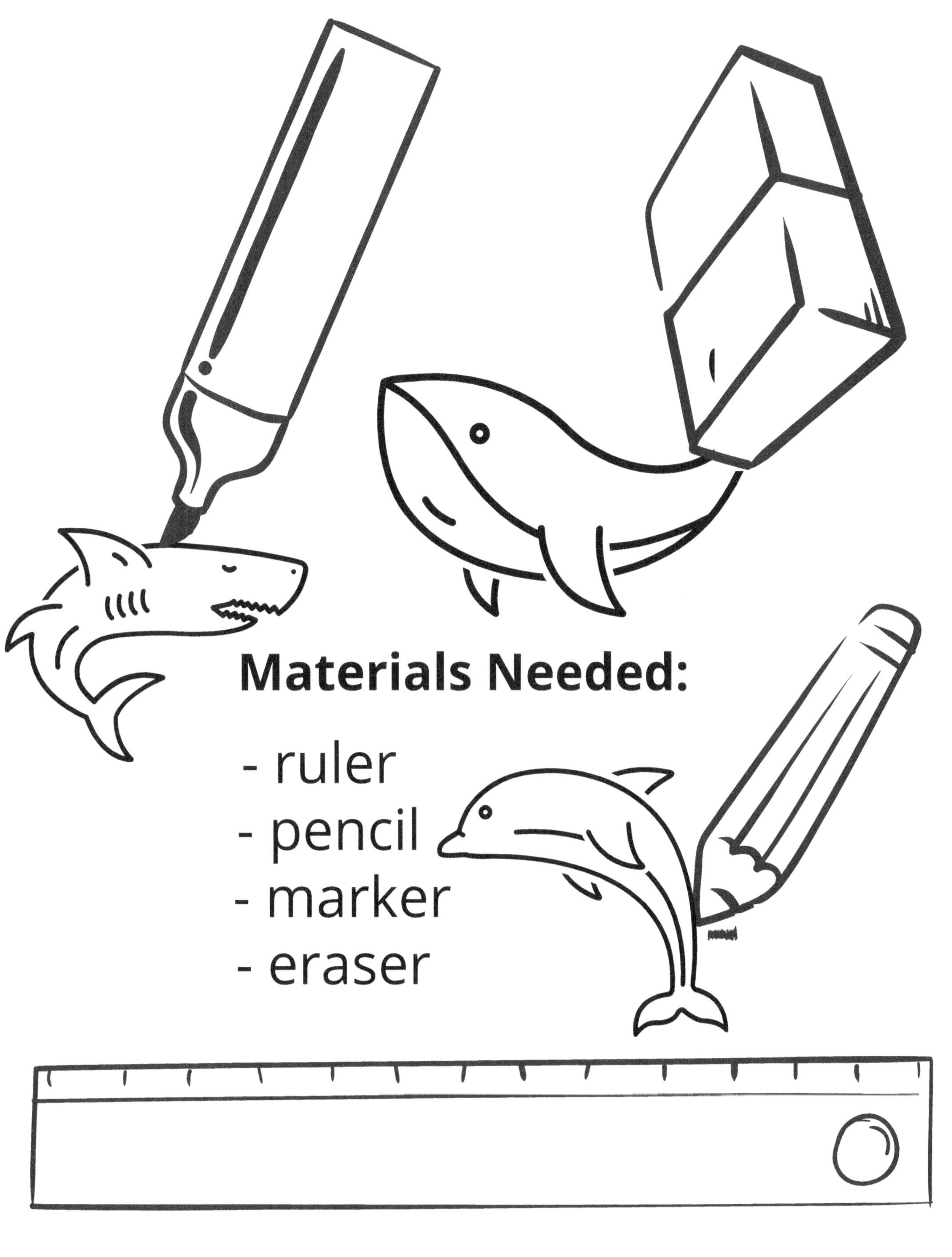

Materials Needed:
- ruler
- pencil
- marker
- eraser

FIRST, LET'S START WITH A TRACING EXERCISE TO IMPROVE OUR SKILLS AND GET USED TO DRAWING, THEN WE'LL MOVE TO THE STEP-BY-STEP DRAWING METHOD.

TRACE AND COLOR

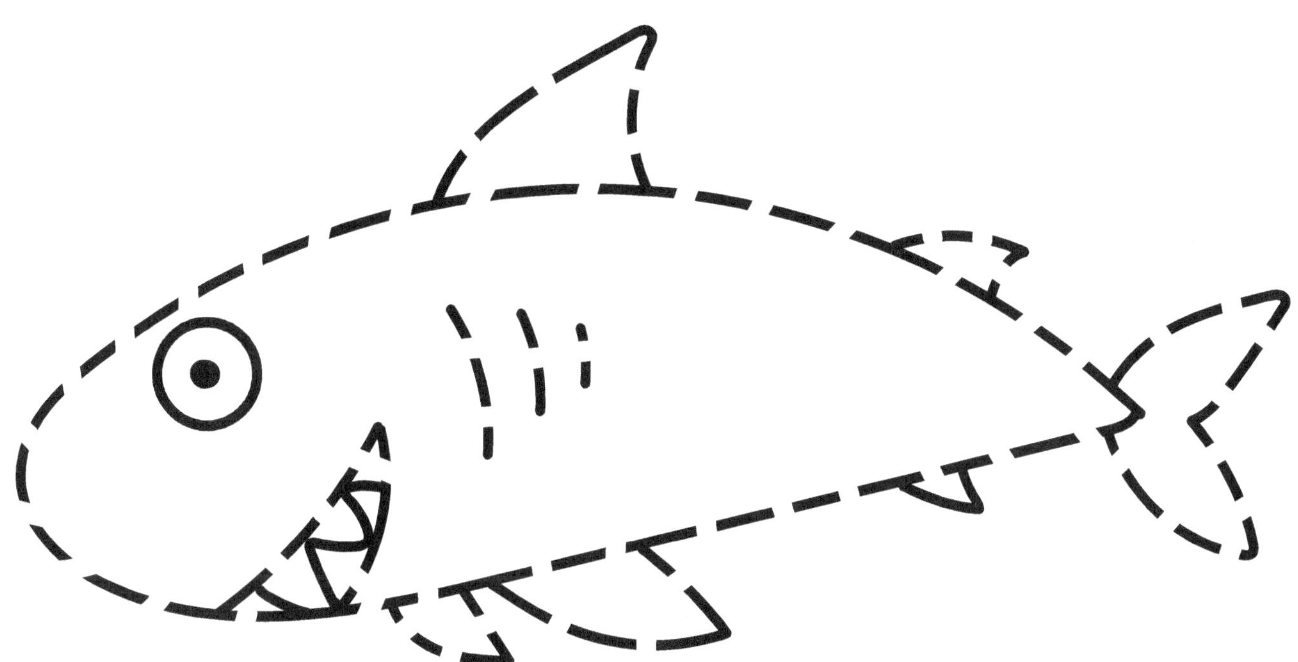

LET'S START DRAWING WITH THE BASE OF OUR FUTURE SHARK

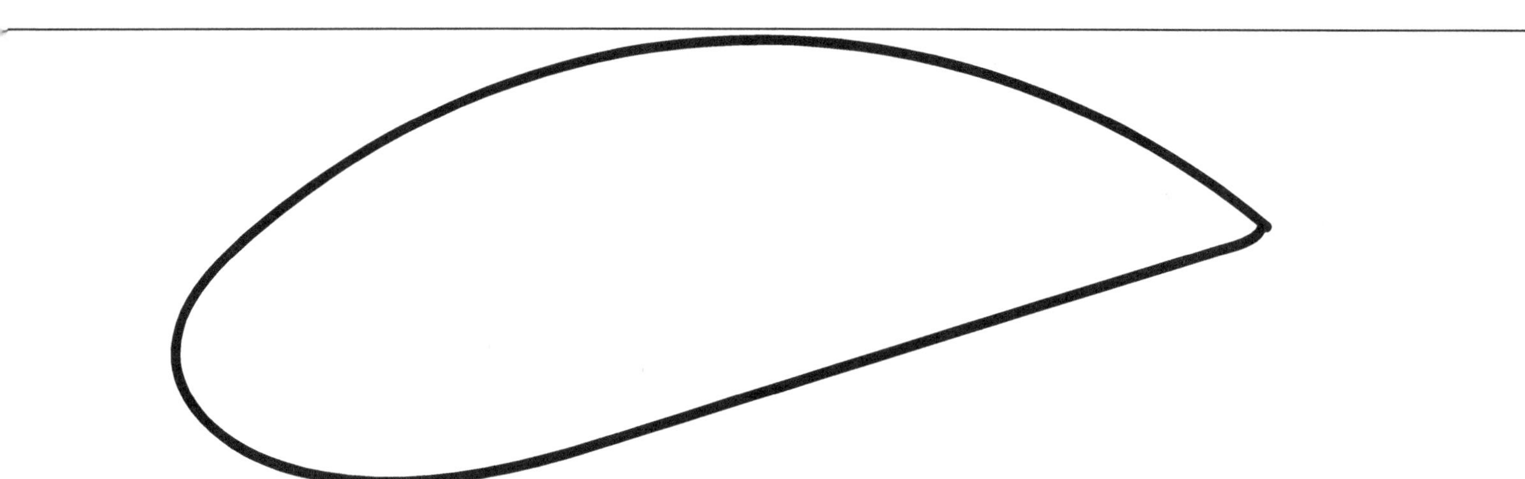

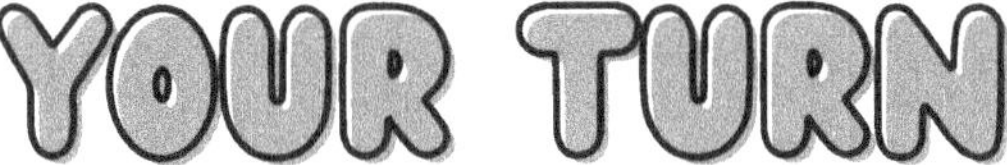

ADD THE TAIL

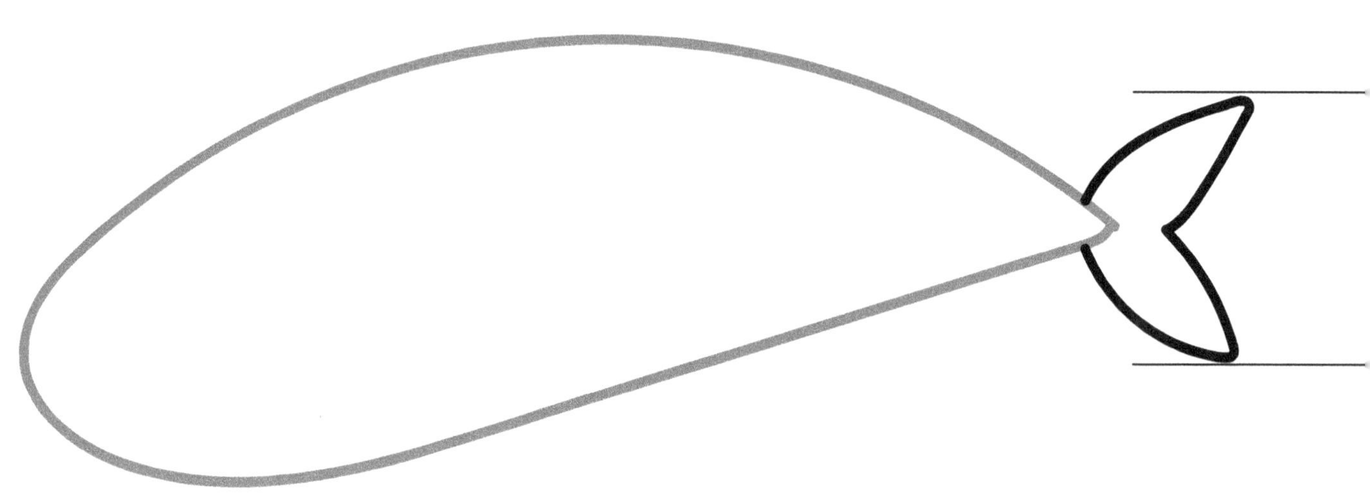

YOUR TURN

A SHARK CAN'T LIVE WITHOUT FINS, SO LET'S DRAW IT.

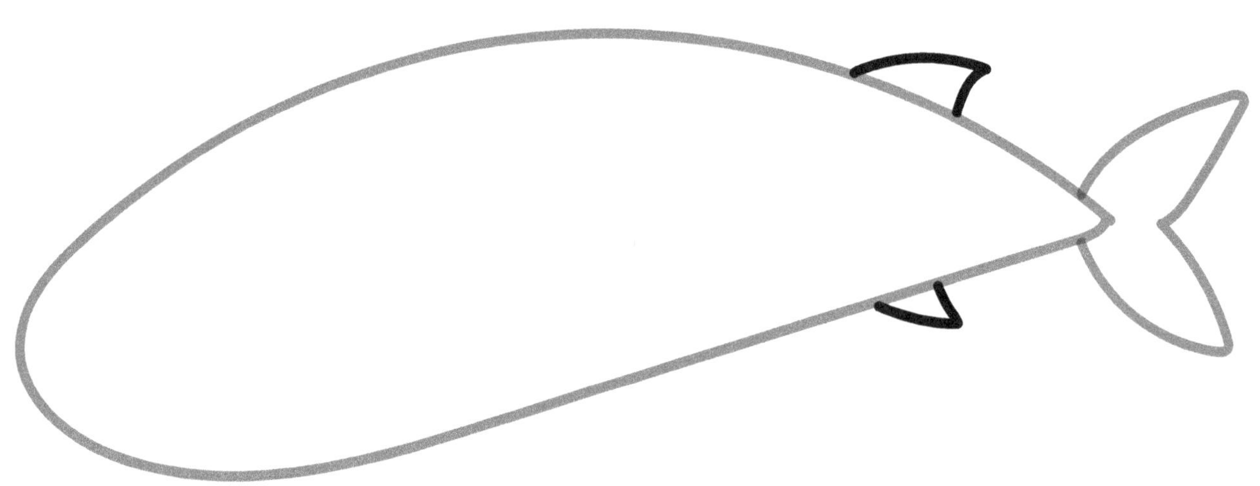

YOUR TURN

CONTINUE DRAWING THE FINS

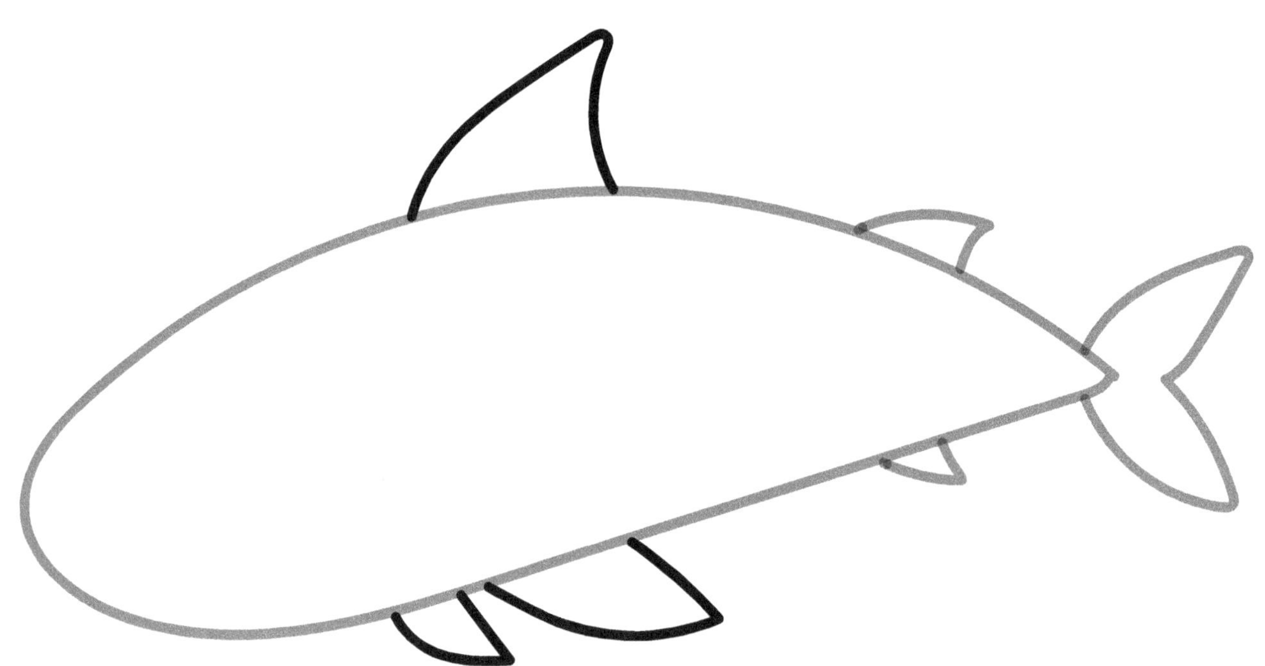

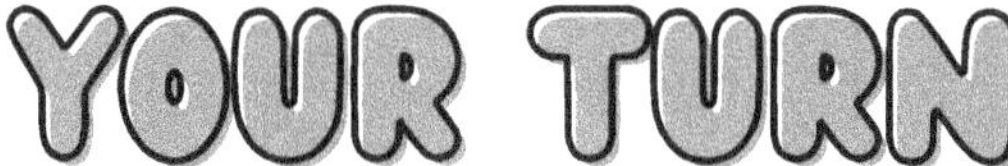

YOUR TURN

NOW, LET'S DRAW THE JAW.

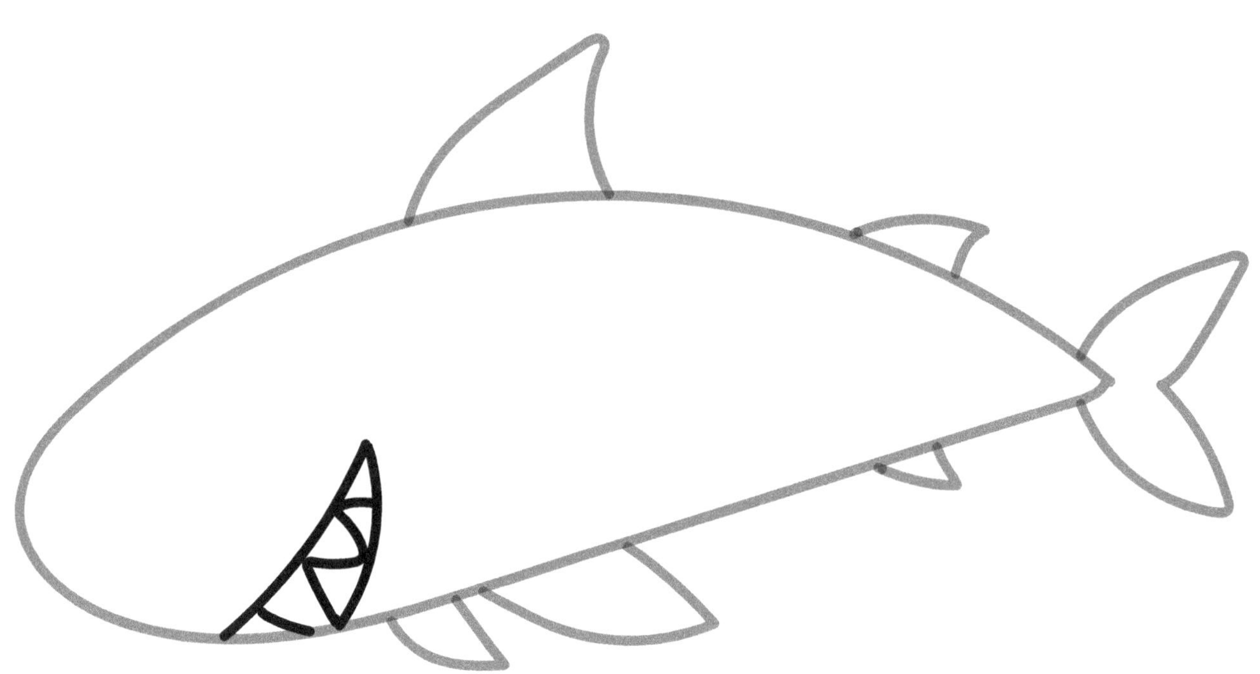

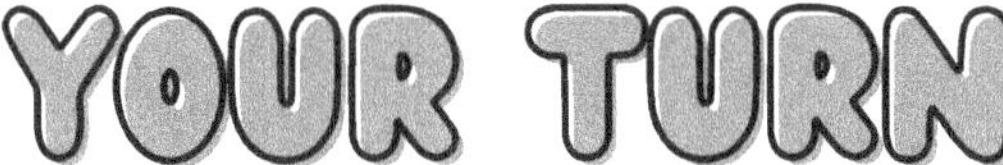
YOUR TURN

COMPLETE DRAWING THE EYE AND GILLS

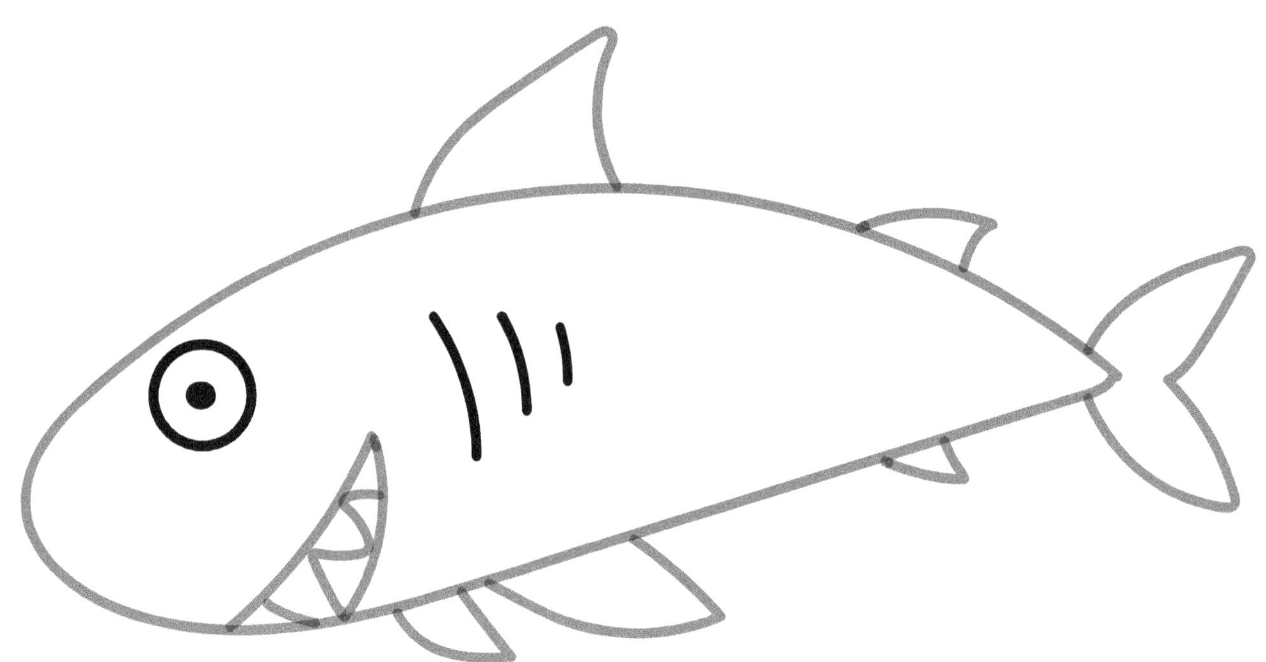

YOUR TURN

NOW, OUR SHARK IS READY, COLOR IT

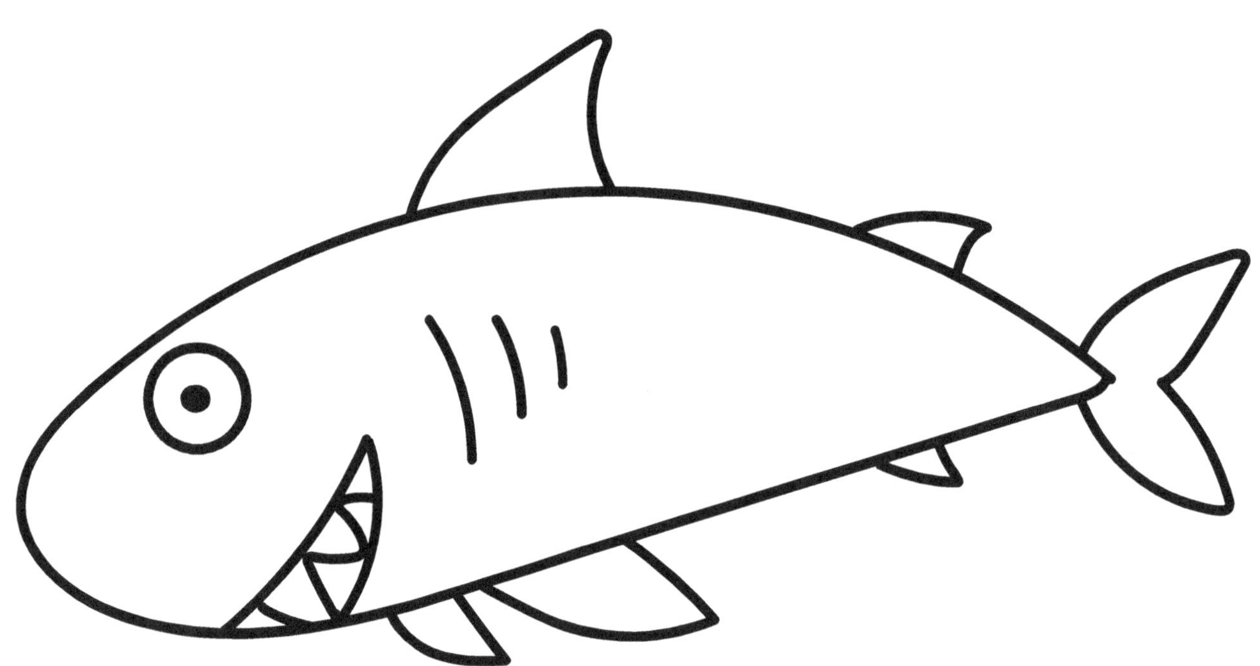

YOUR TURN

NOW LET'S DRAW ANOTHER SEA
ANIMAL!
WHAT ABOUT ONE OF THE BIGGEST
CREATURES IN THE OCEAN!
YES! LET'S DRAW A WHALE

TRACE AND COLOR

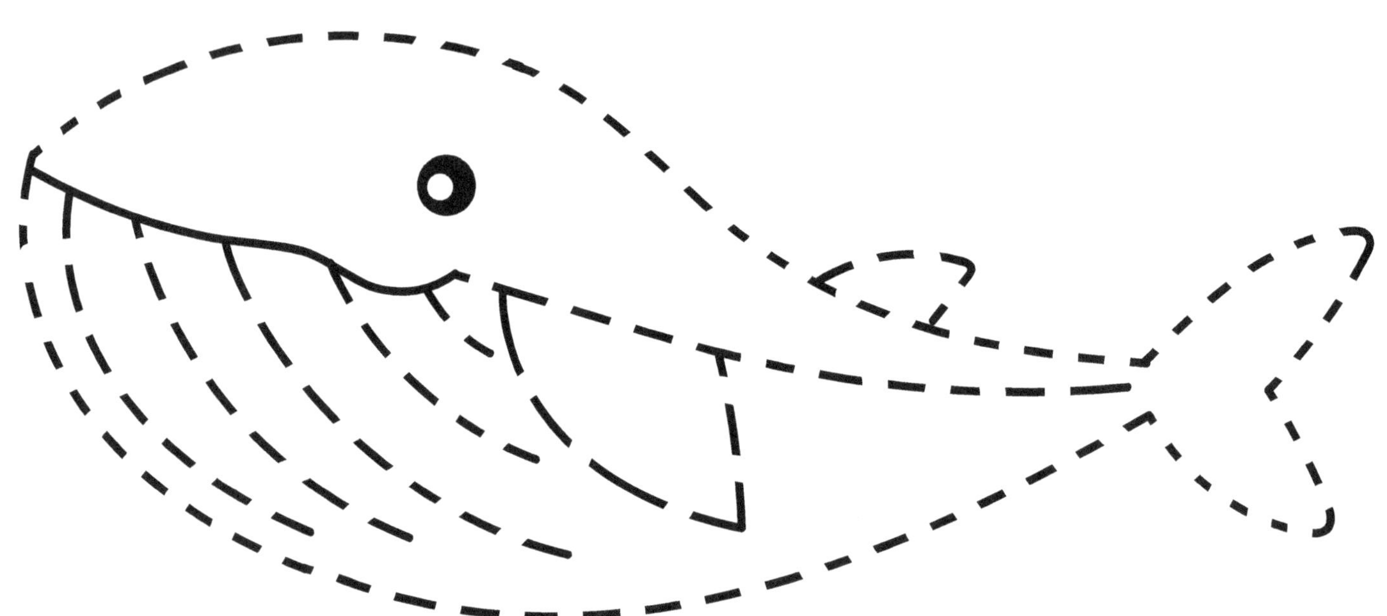

LET'S START DRAWING WITH THE HEAD OF OUR WHALE

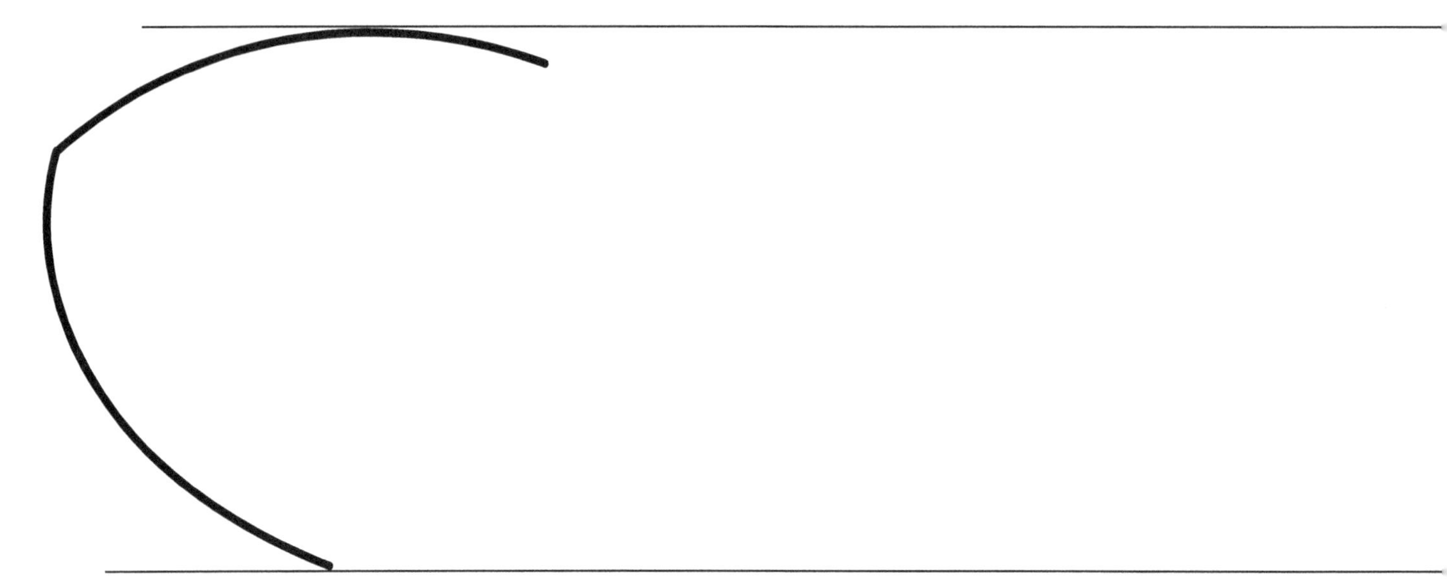

YOUR TURN

COMPLETE THE BODY

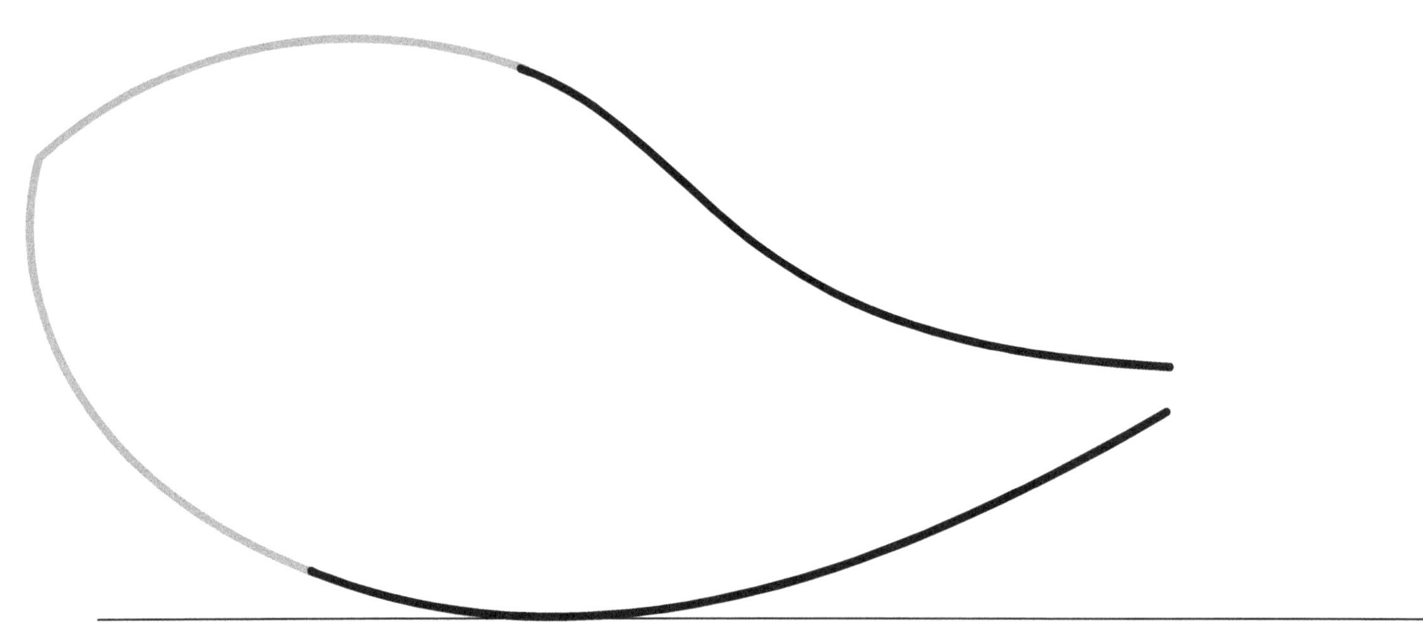

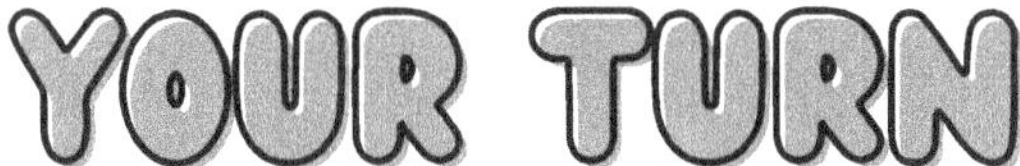
YOUR TURN

ADD THE TAIL

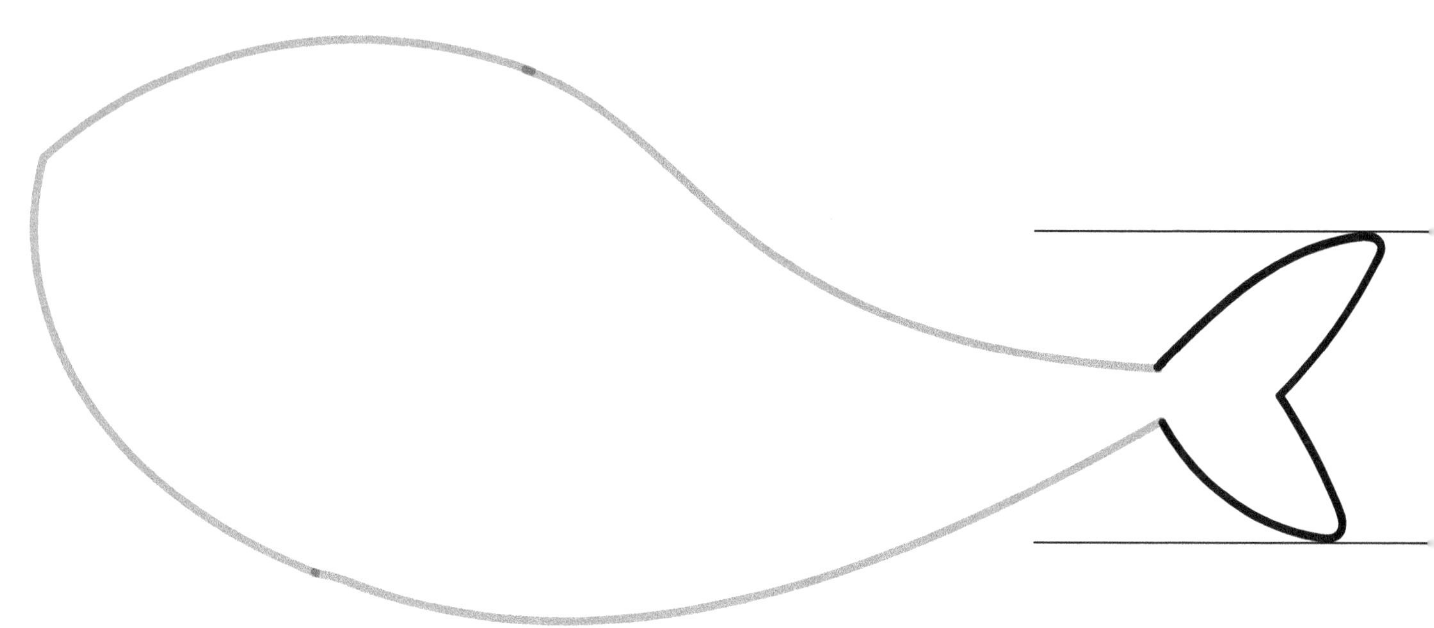

YOUR TURN

DRAW A SIMPLE FINS

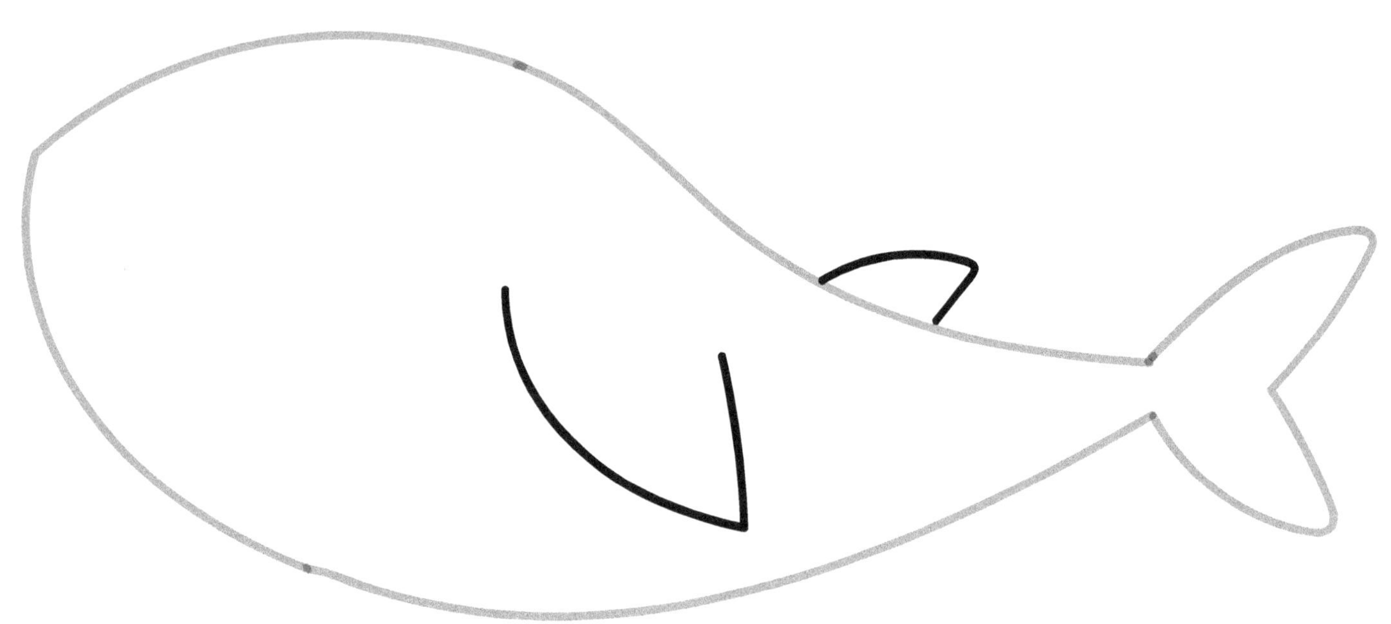

YOUR TURN

DRAW THE WHALE EYE AND MOUTH

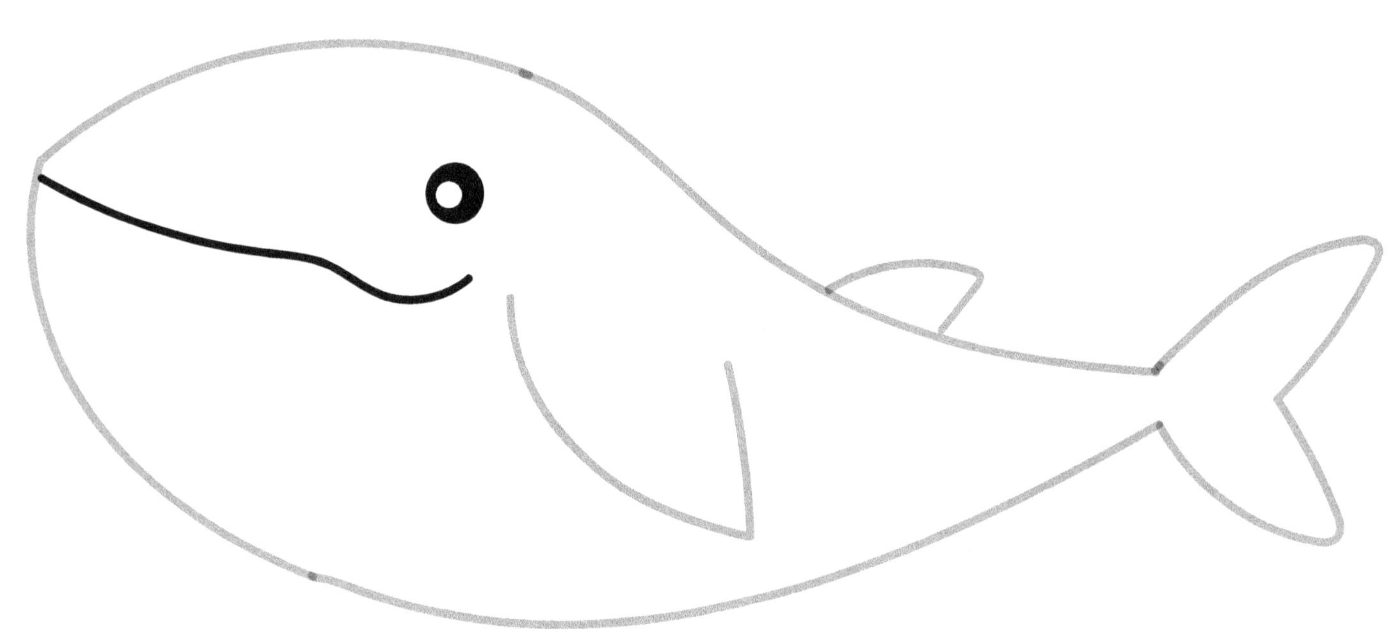

YOUR TURN

DRAW LINES ON THE BELLY

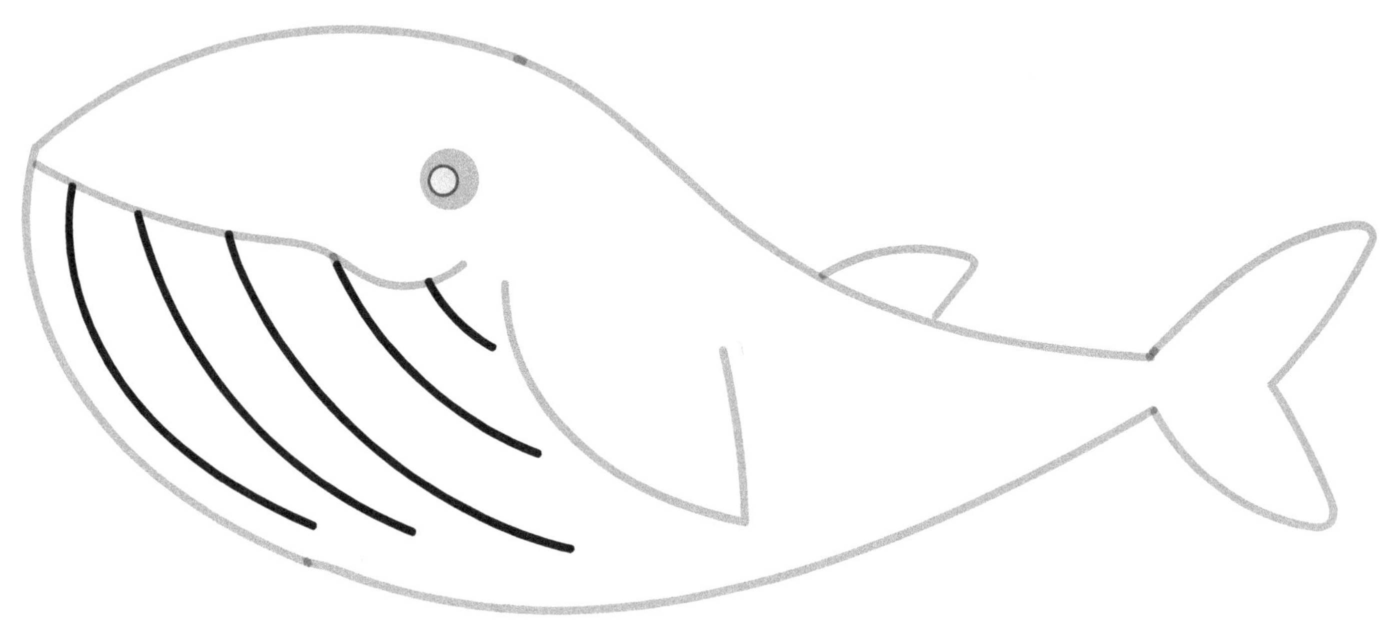

YOUR TURN

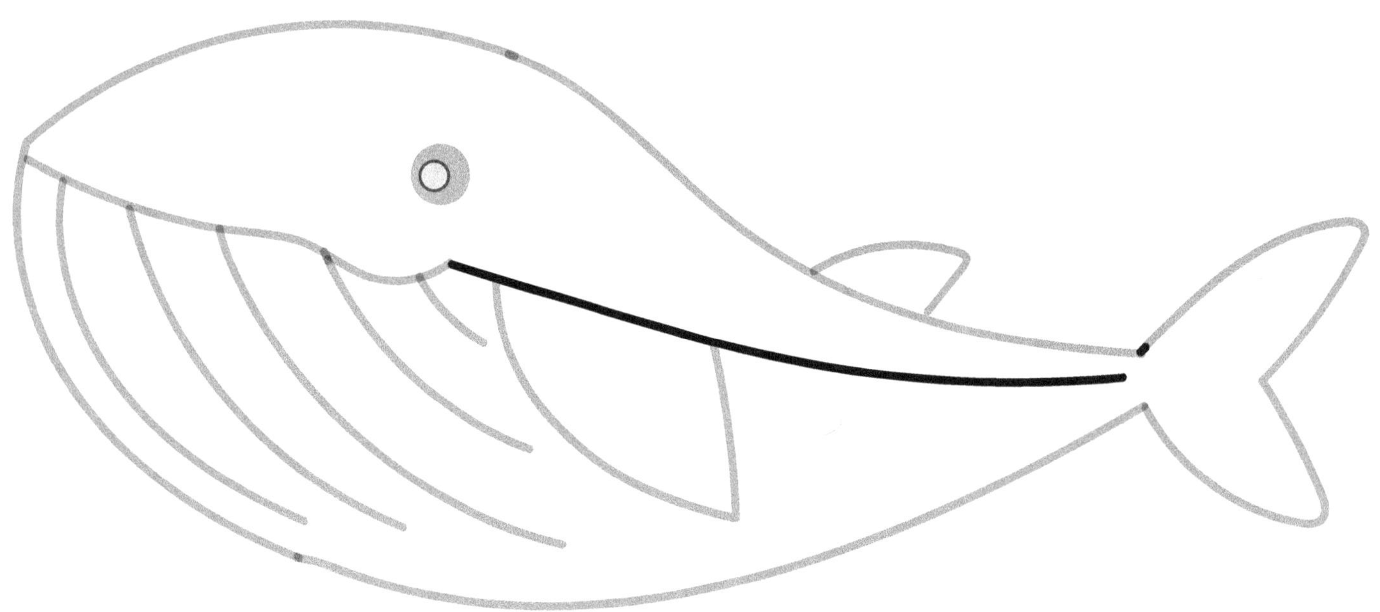

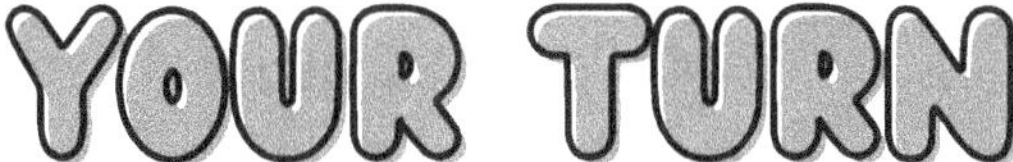
YOUR TURN

OUR WHALE IS READY NOW! COLOR IT :)

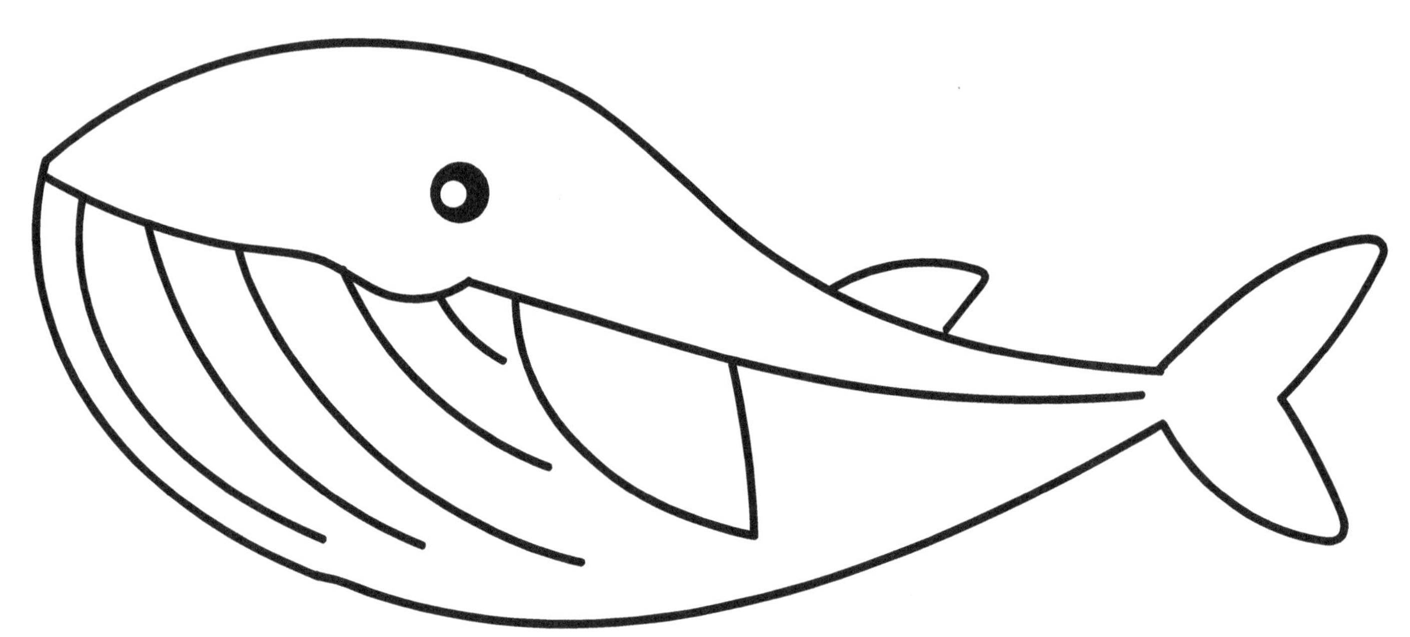

WE MUST NOT FORGET TO DRAW A FISH
IT'S ONE OF THE EASIEST ANIMALS TO
DRAW

DRAW THE OUTLINE OF THE FISH

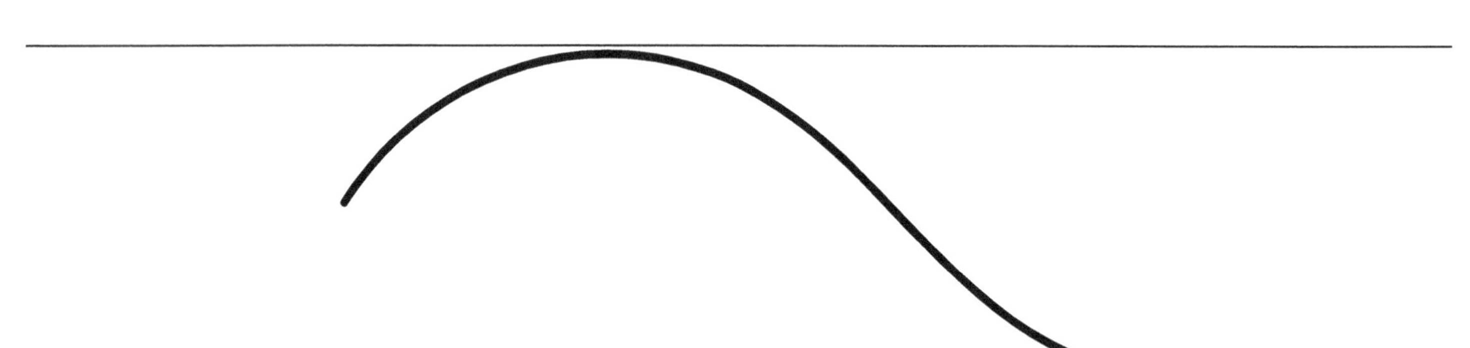

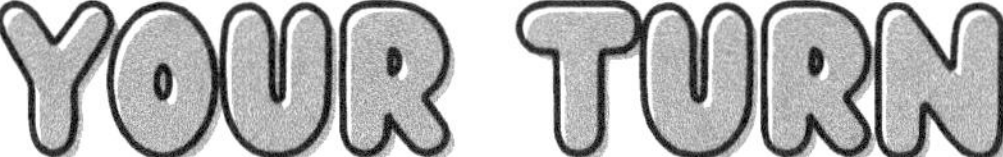

YOUR TURN

DRAW THE OUTLINE OF THE FISH

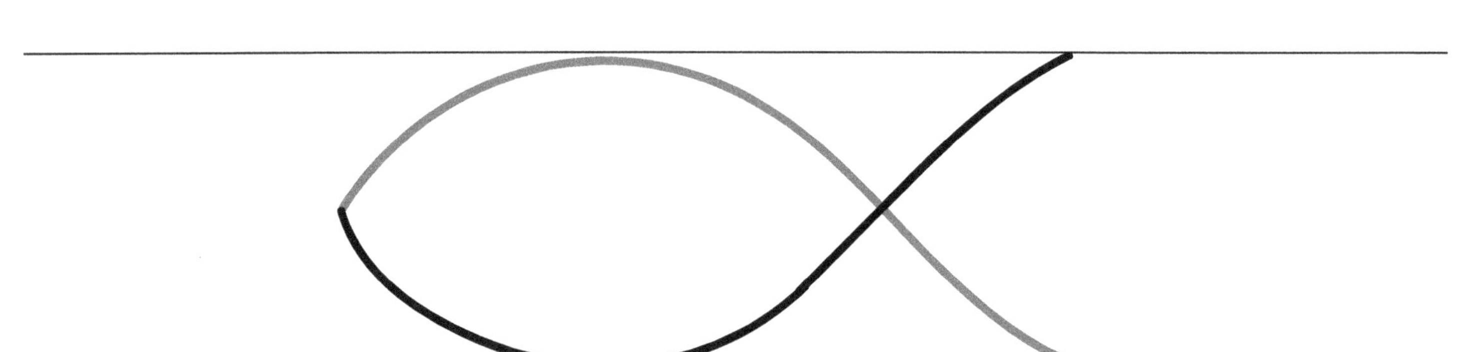

YOUR TURN

DRAW THE TAIL

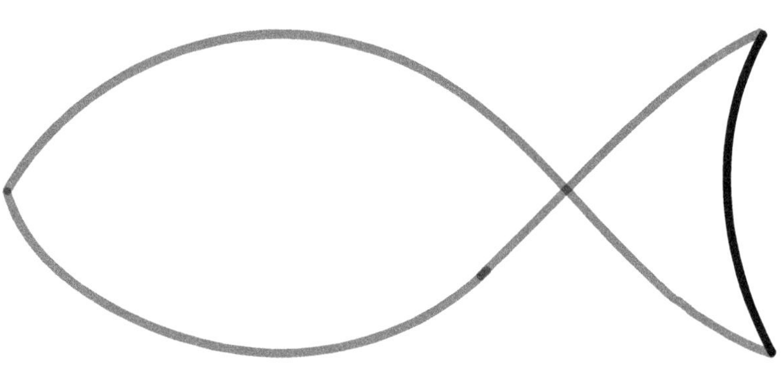

YOUR TURN

DRAW THE EYE AND THE MOUTH

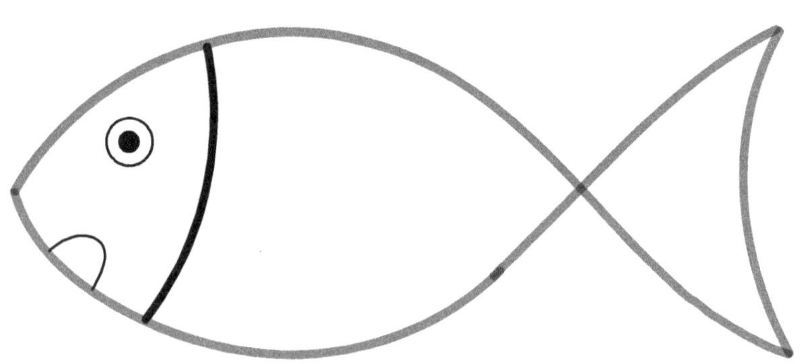

YOUR TURN

DRAW THE FINS

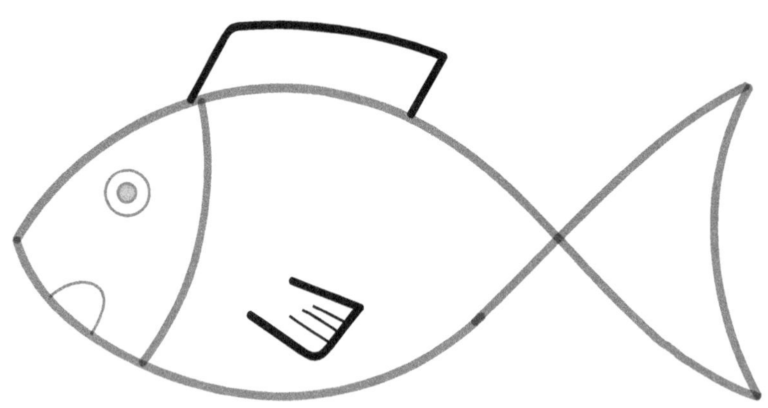

YOUR TURN

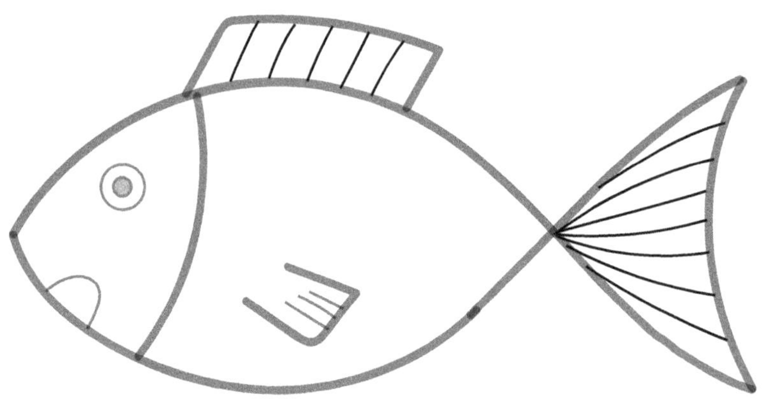

YOUR TURN

LET'S COLOR OUR FISH

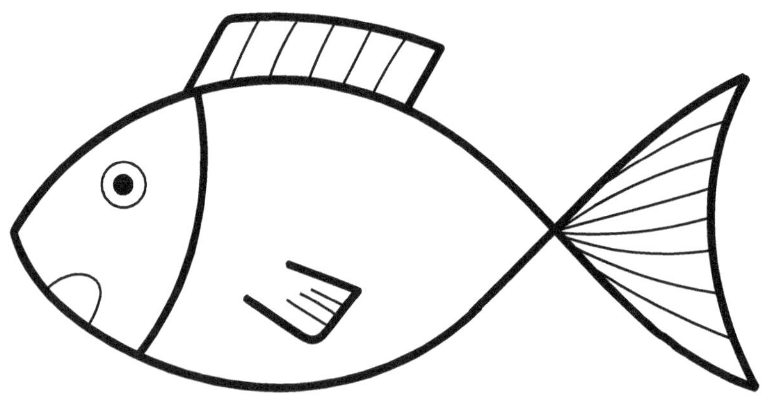

YOUR TURN

NOW, LET'S MOVE TO THE BEST AND MOST FAMOUS ANIMAL IN THE SEA

- THE DOLPHIN -

TRACE AND COLOR

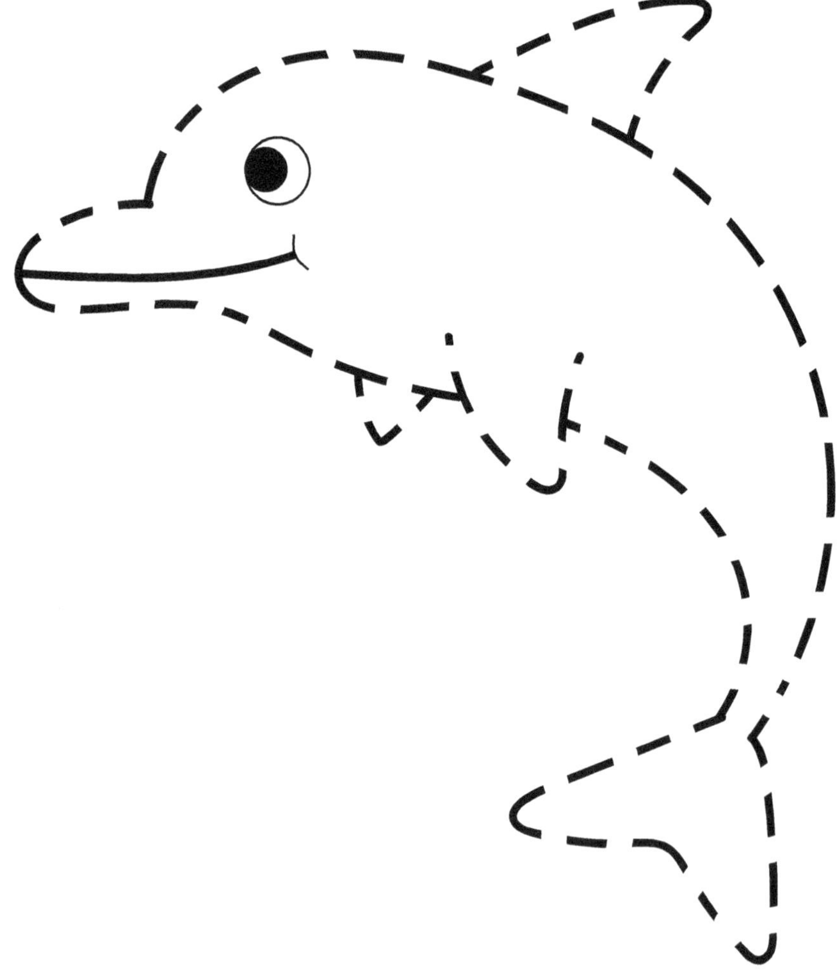

FIRST DRAW THE DOLPHIN'S HEAD

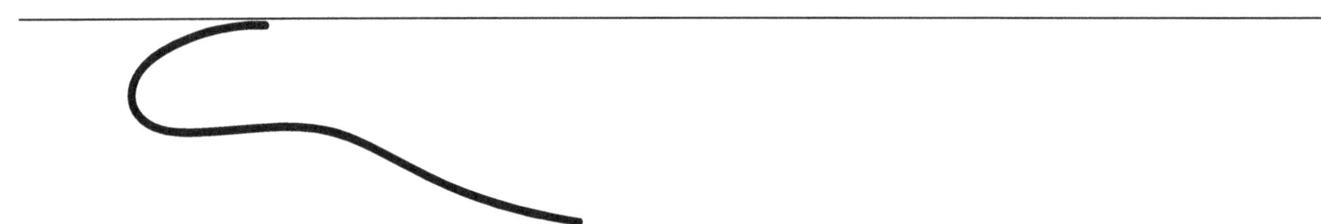

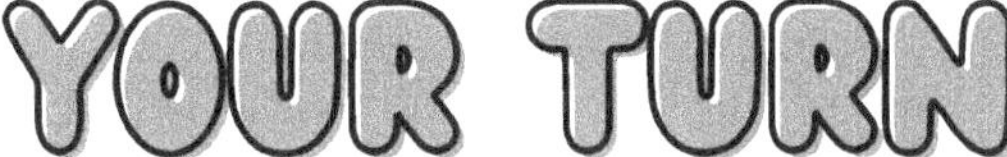

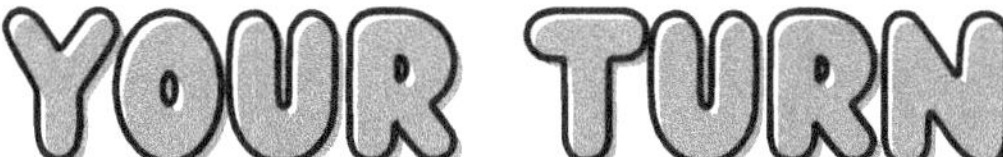

YOUR TURN

DRAW THE DOLPHIN BODY

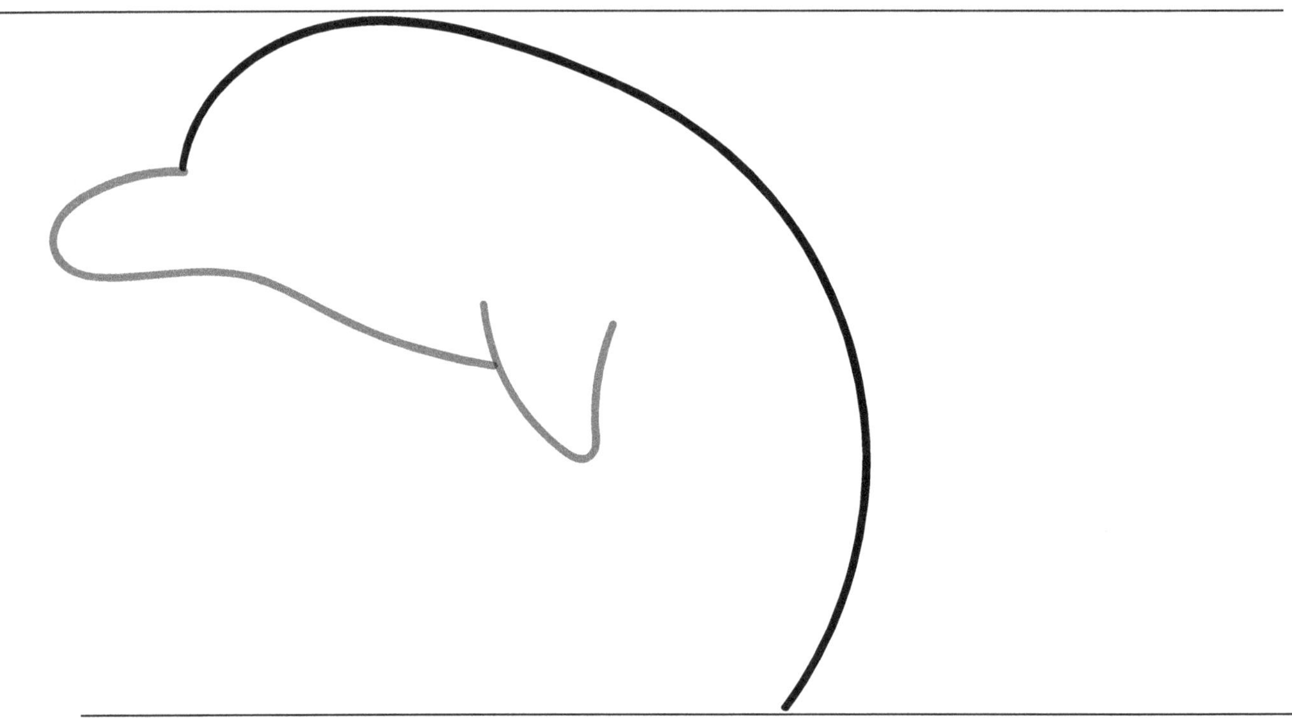

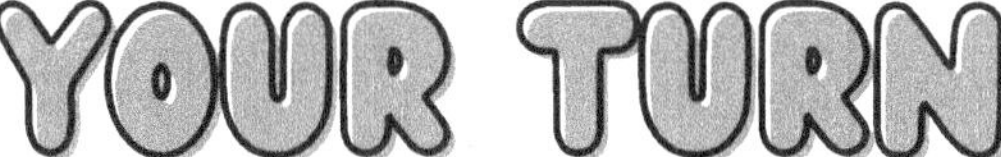

DRAW THE EYE AND THE MOUTH

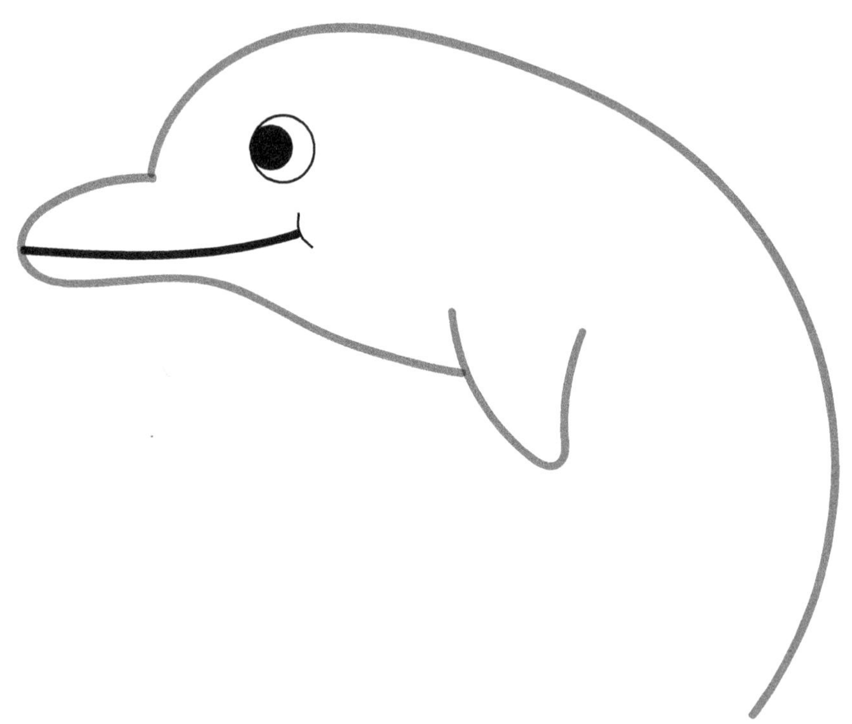

YOUR TURN

COMPLETE DRAWING THE BODY

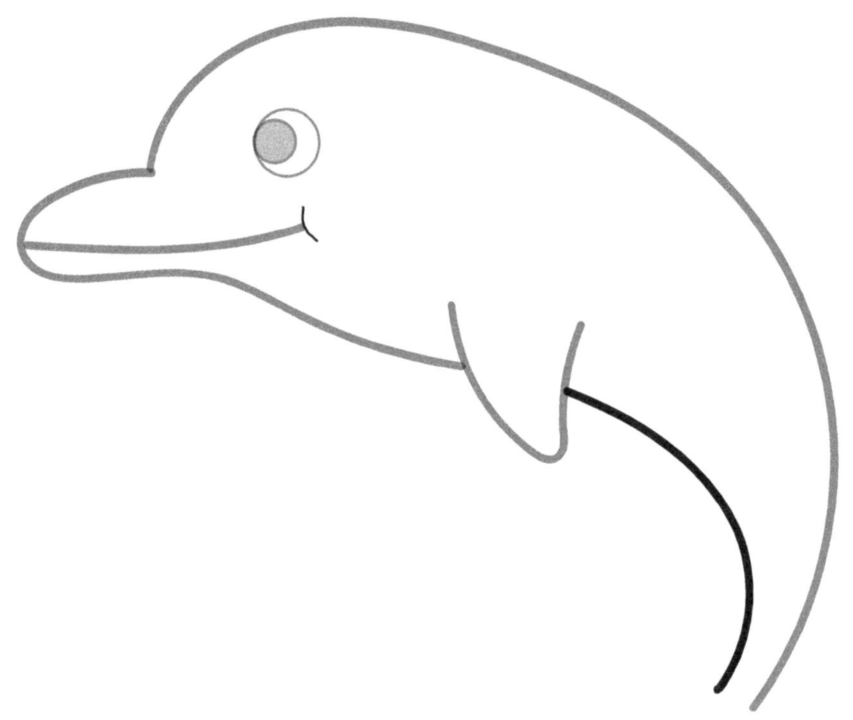

YOUR TURN

DRAW THE FINS

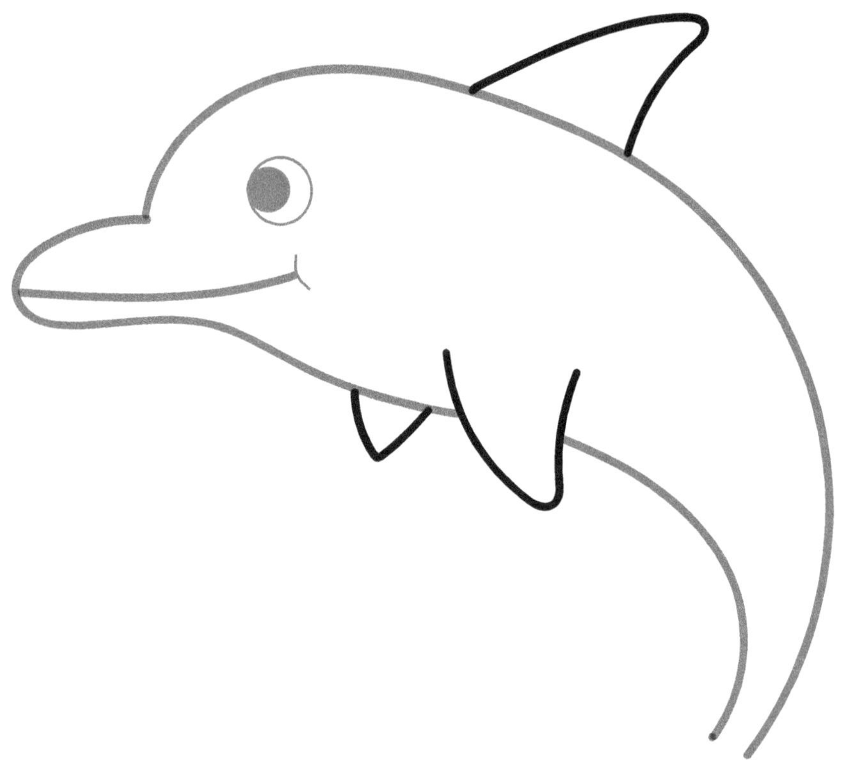

YOUR TURN

DRAW THE TAIL

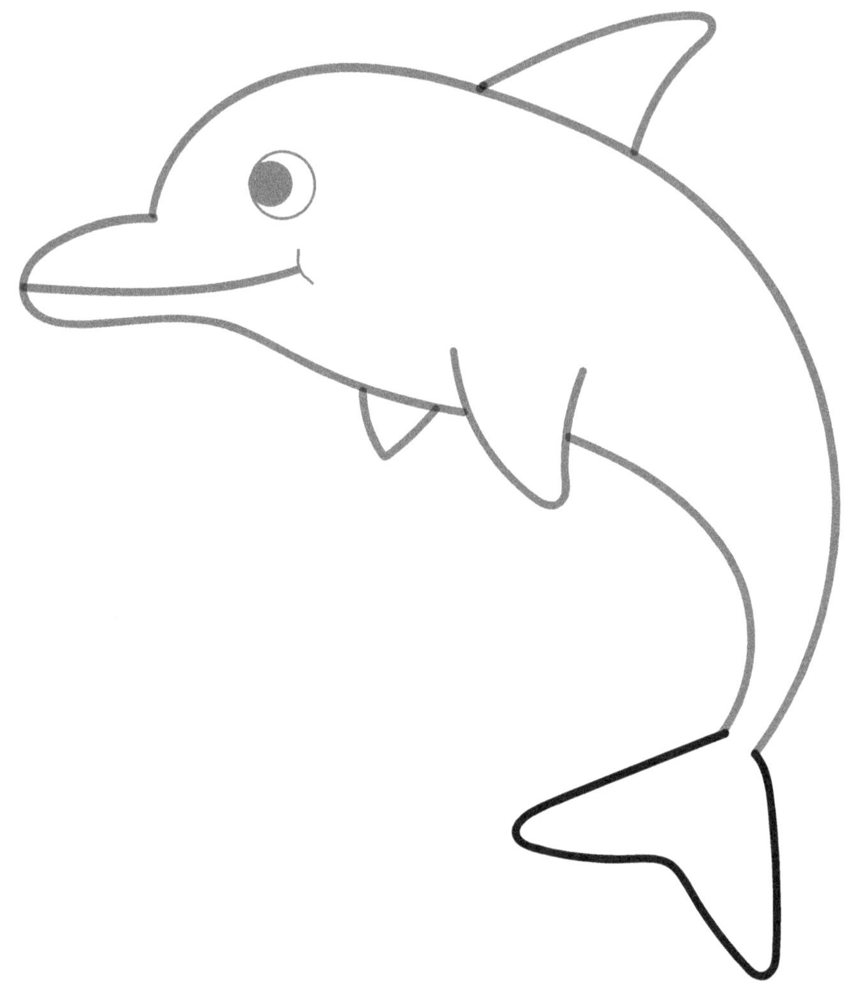

YOUR TURN

NOW IT'S COLORING TIME !

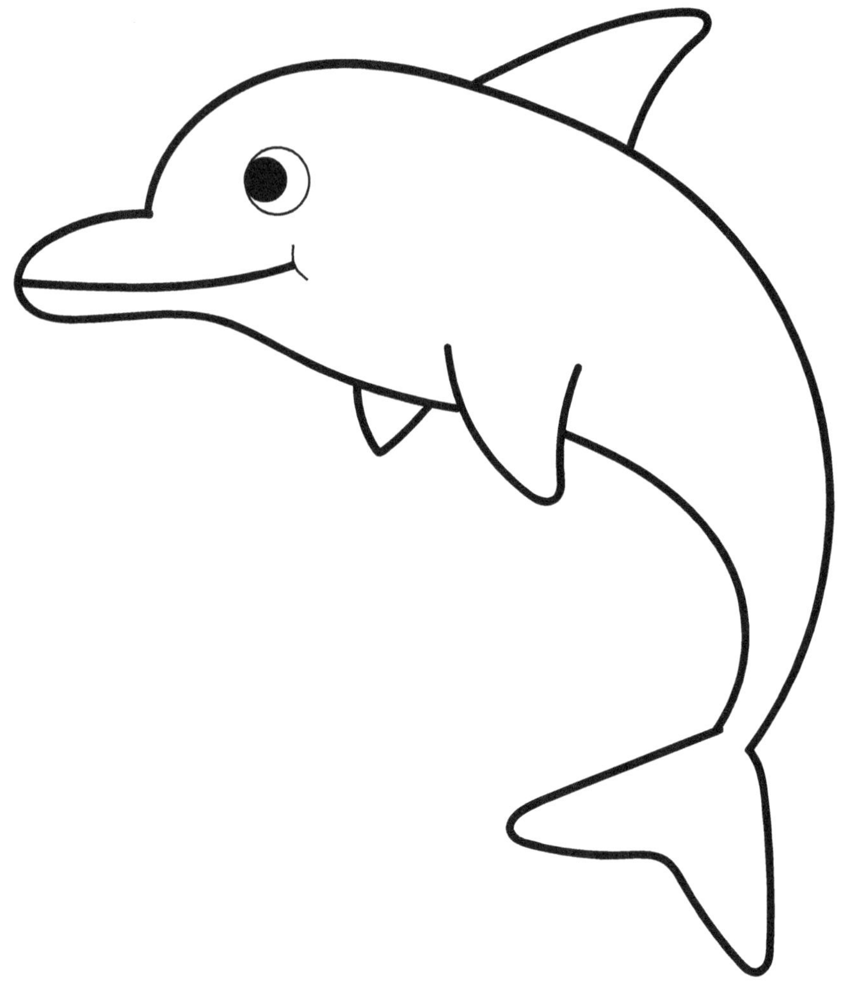

DID YOU KNOW THAT DOLPHINS HAVE
BIG BRAINS?
IT'S ONE OF THE SMARTEST ANIMALS
IN THE WORLD!

NOW, LET'S TRY SOMETHING DIFFERENT
LET'S DRAW A TURTLE

TRACE AND COLOR

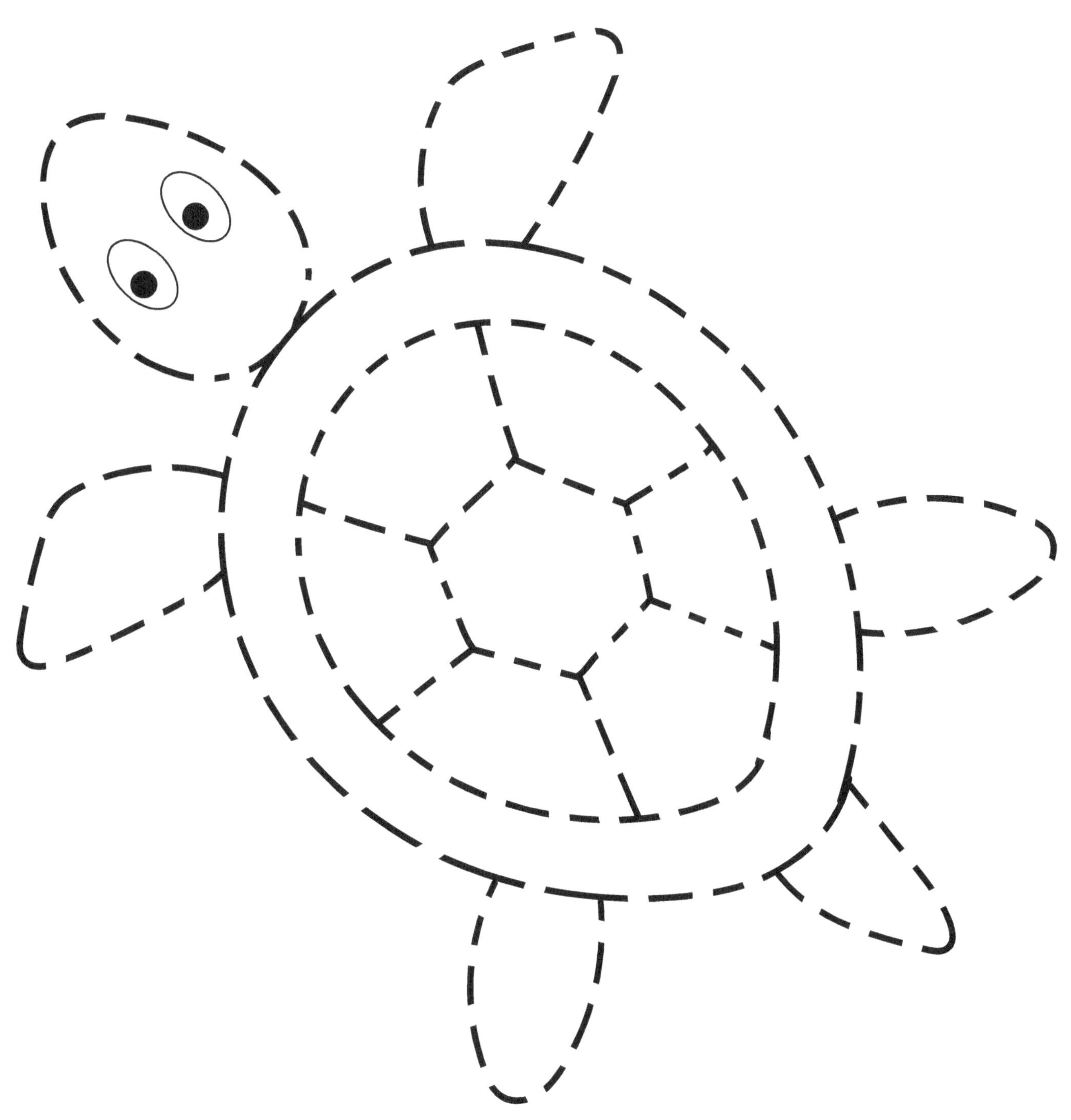

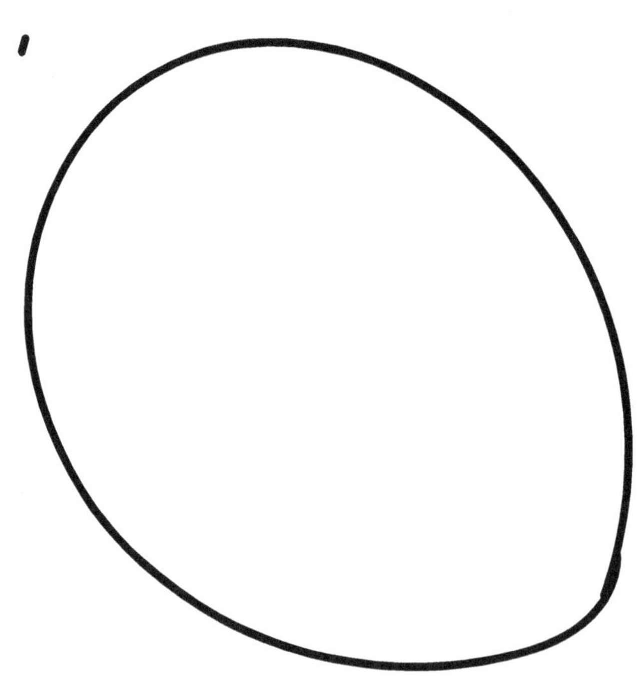

YOUR TURN

OUTSIDE THE OVAL SHAPE, DRAW ANOTHER ONE.

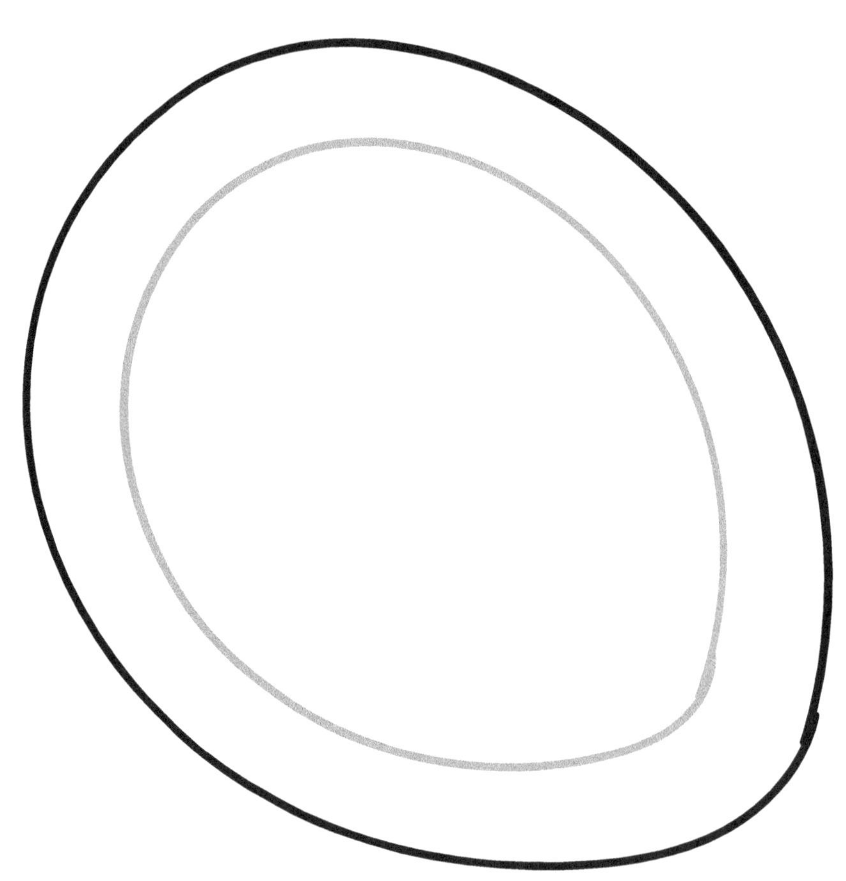

YOUR TURN

DRAW THE HEAD AND THE TAIL.

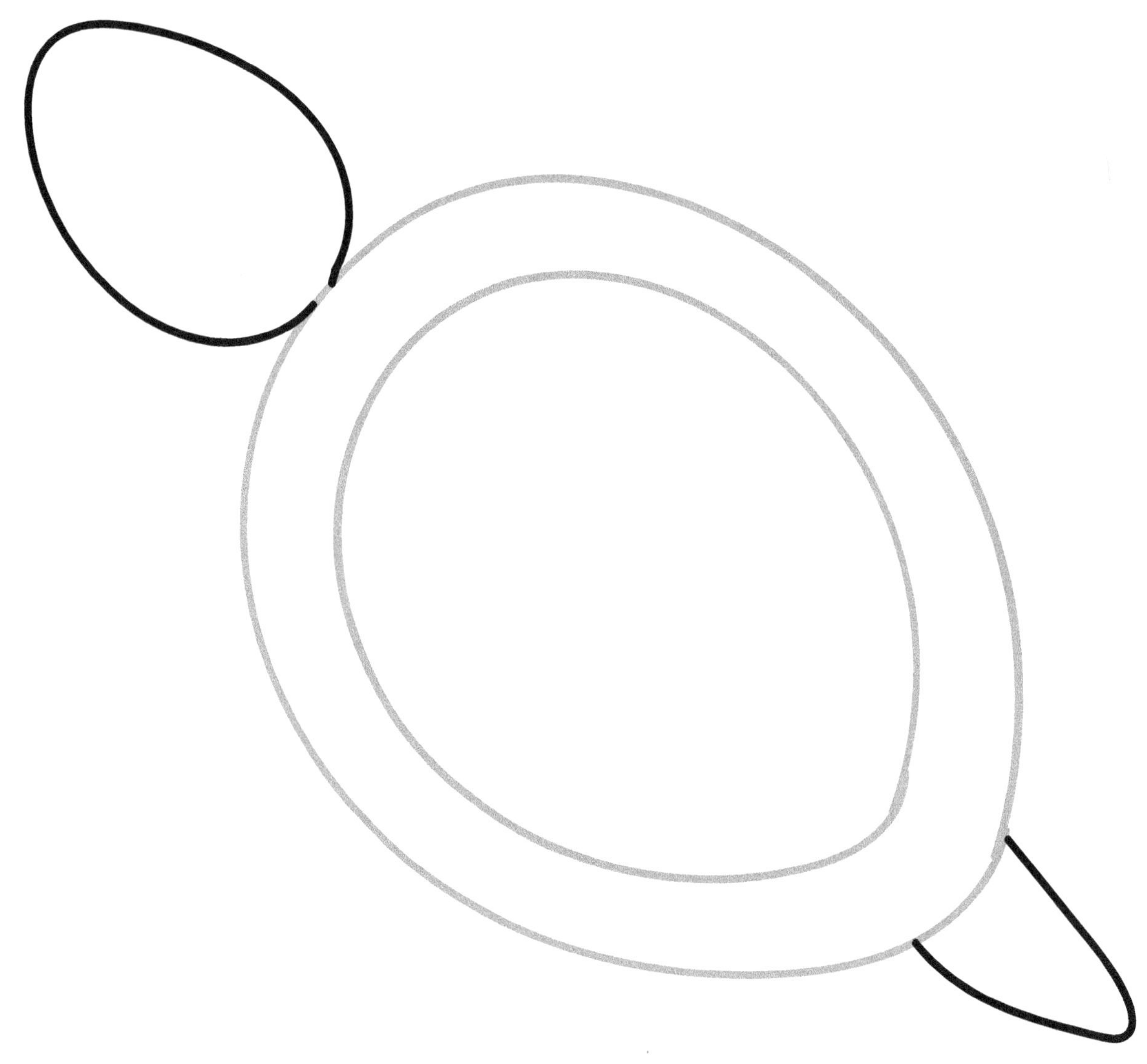

YOUR TURN

DRAW THE LEGS

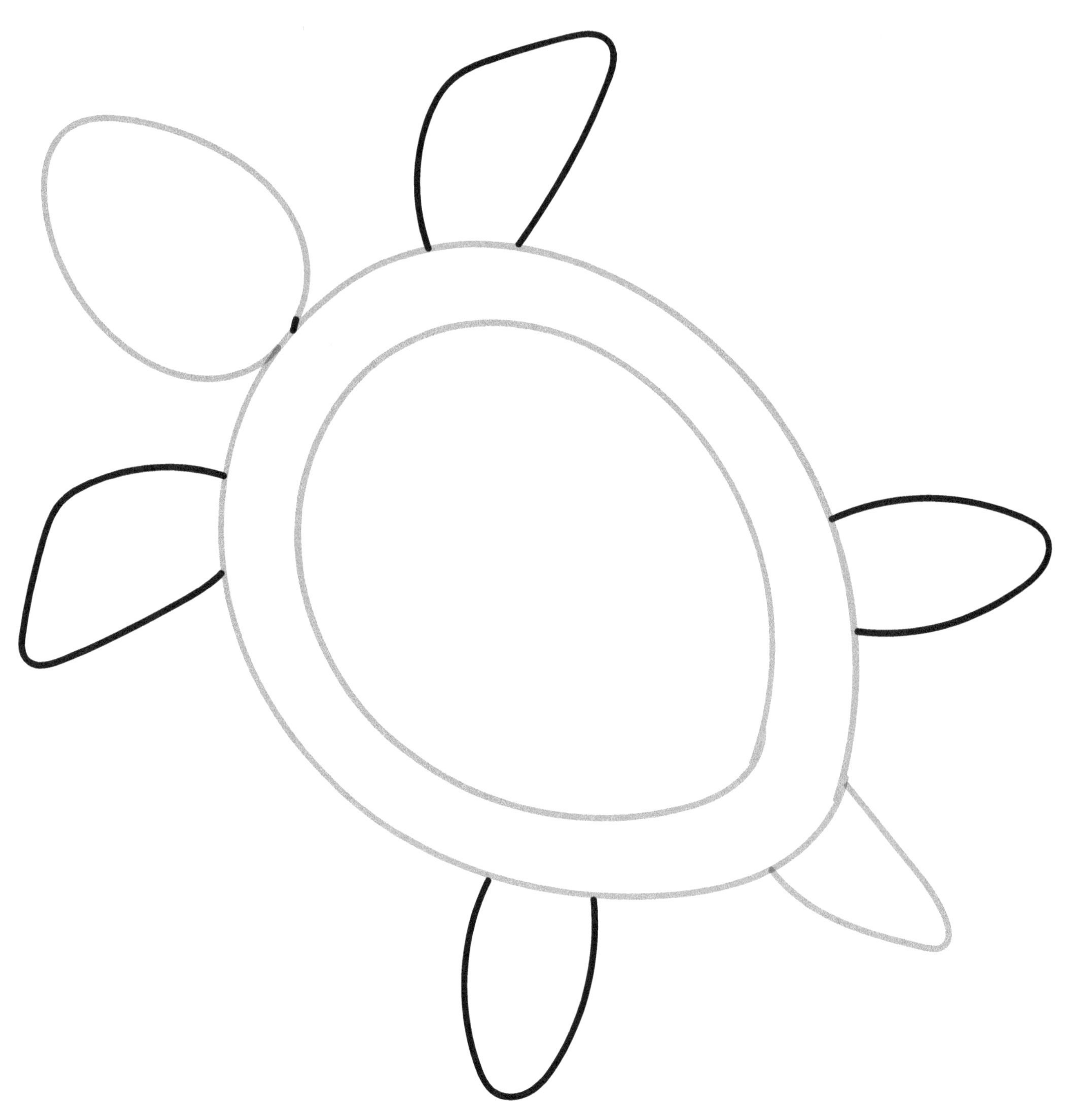

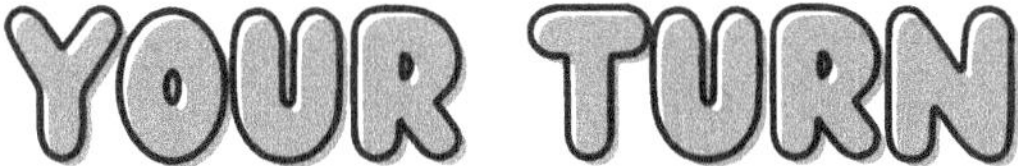

YOUR TURN

NOW ADD SOME DETAILS TO THE SHELL AND DRAW THE EYES

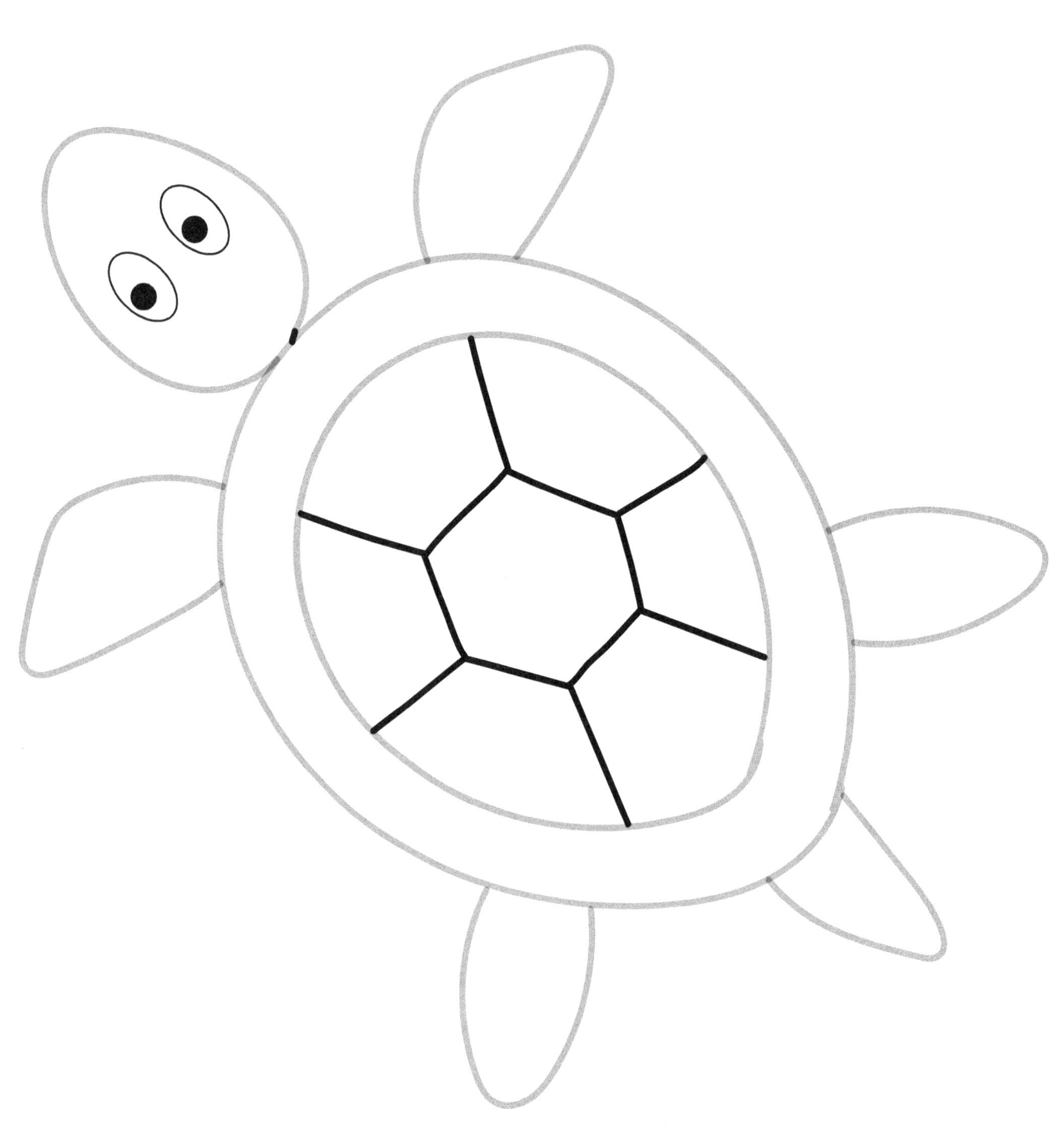

YOUR TURN

HERE IS OUR TURTLE, COLOR IT

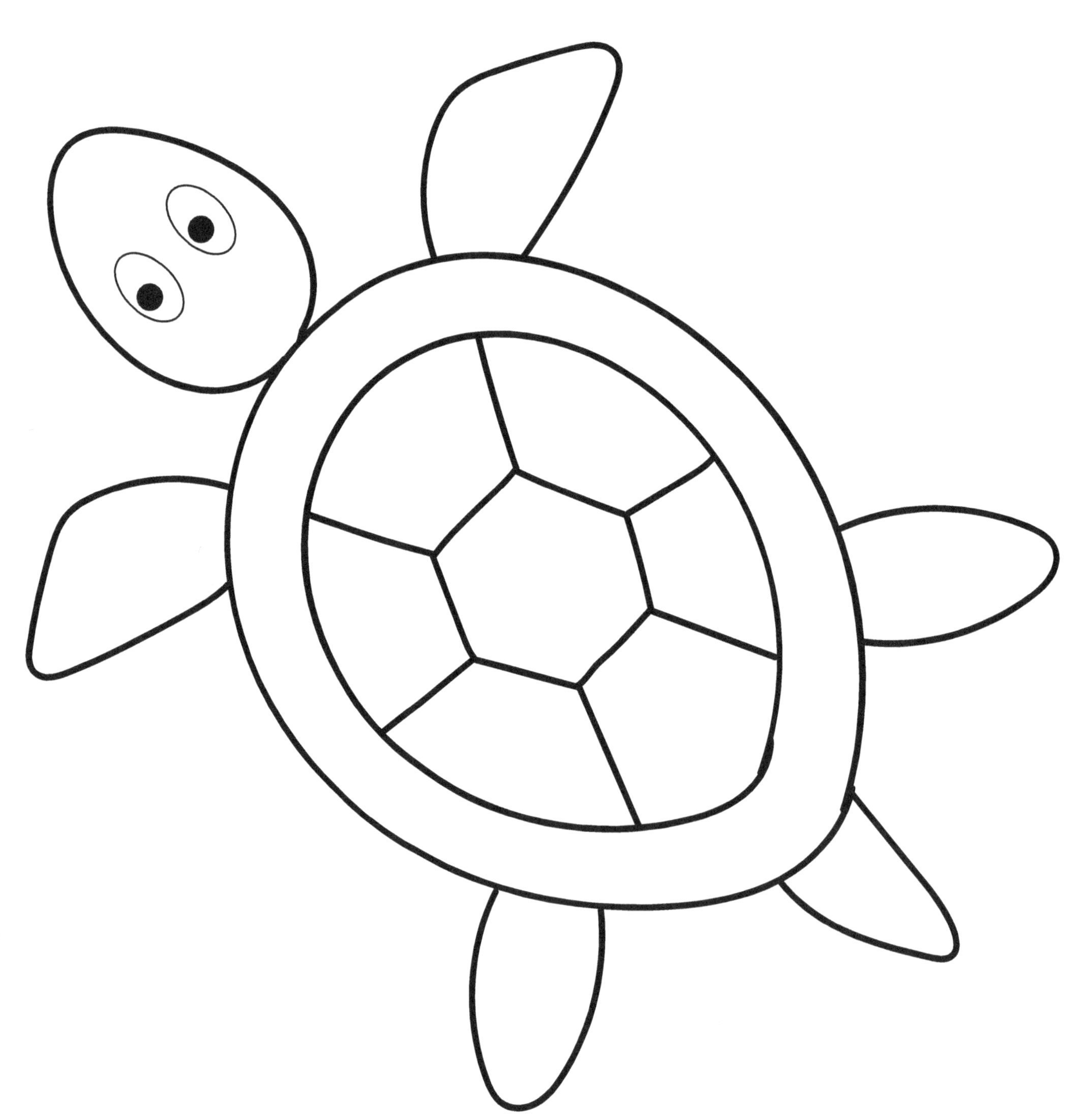

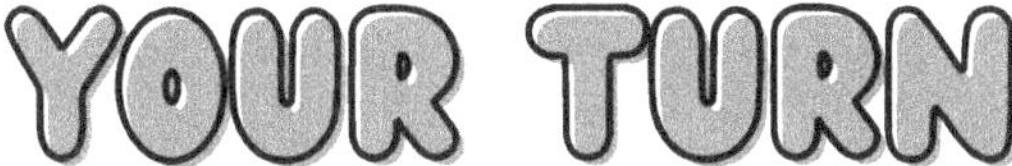

YOUR TURN

COLORING PAGES

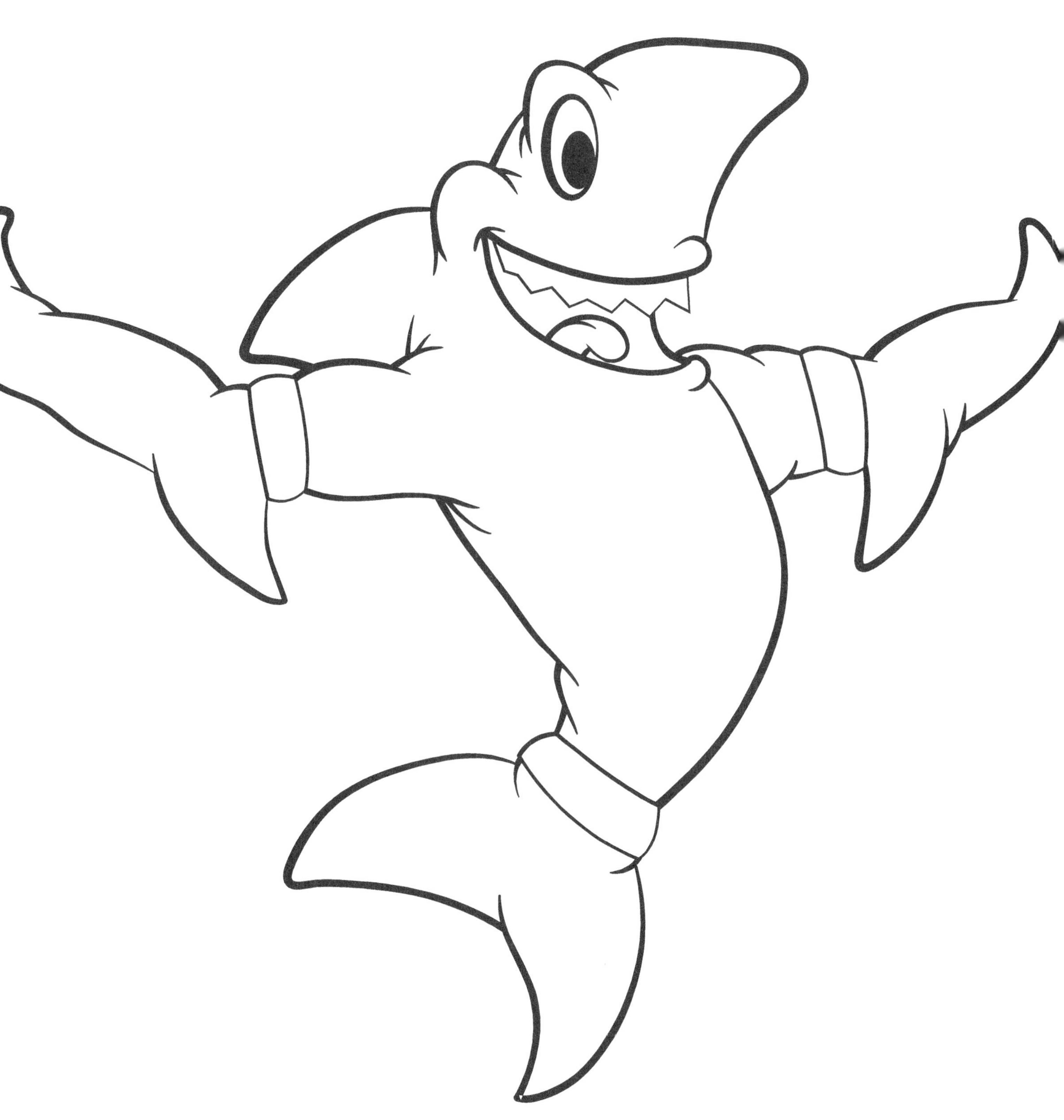

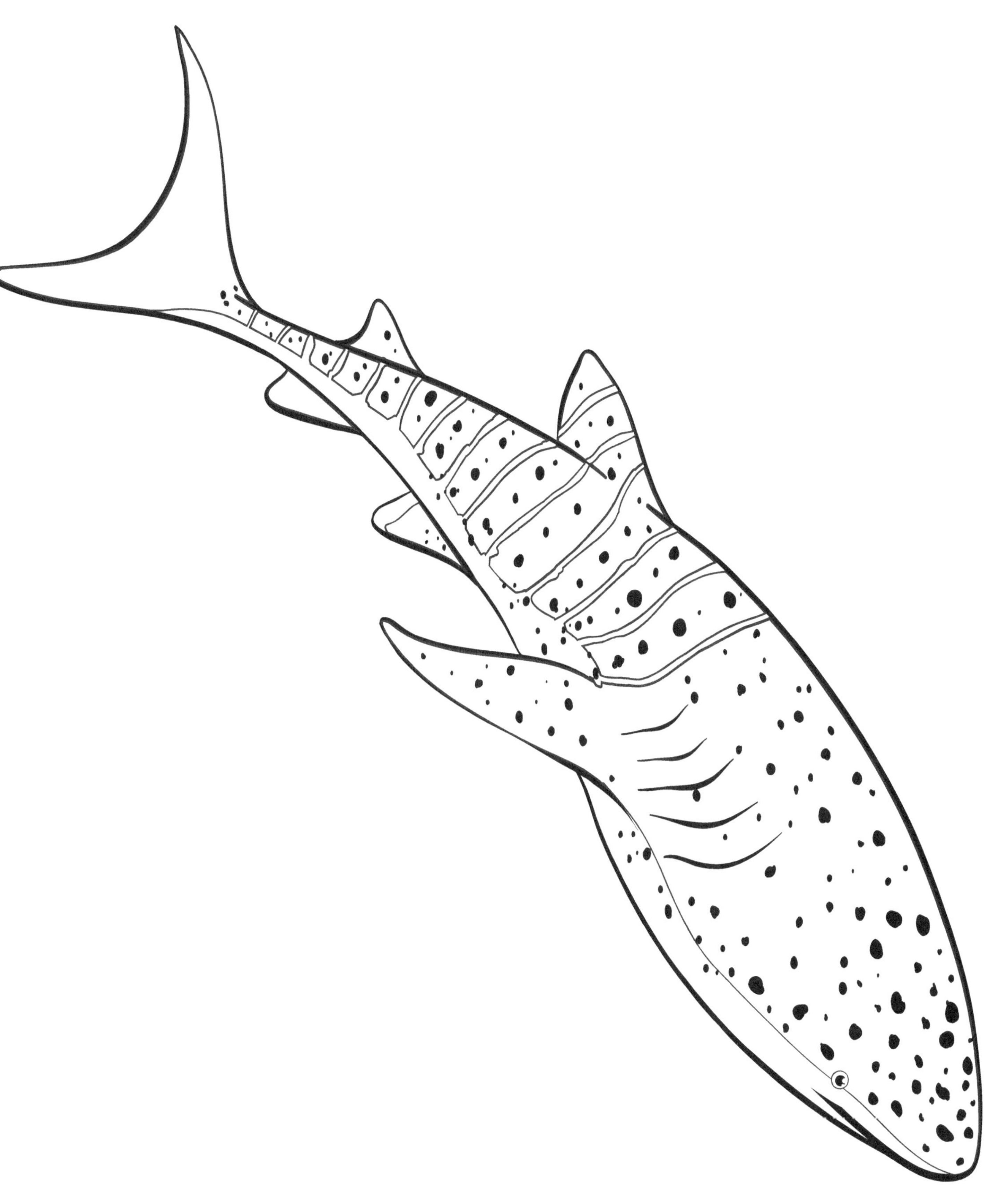

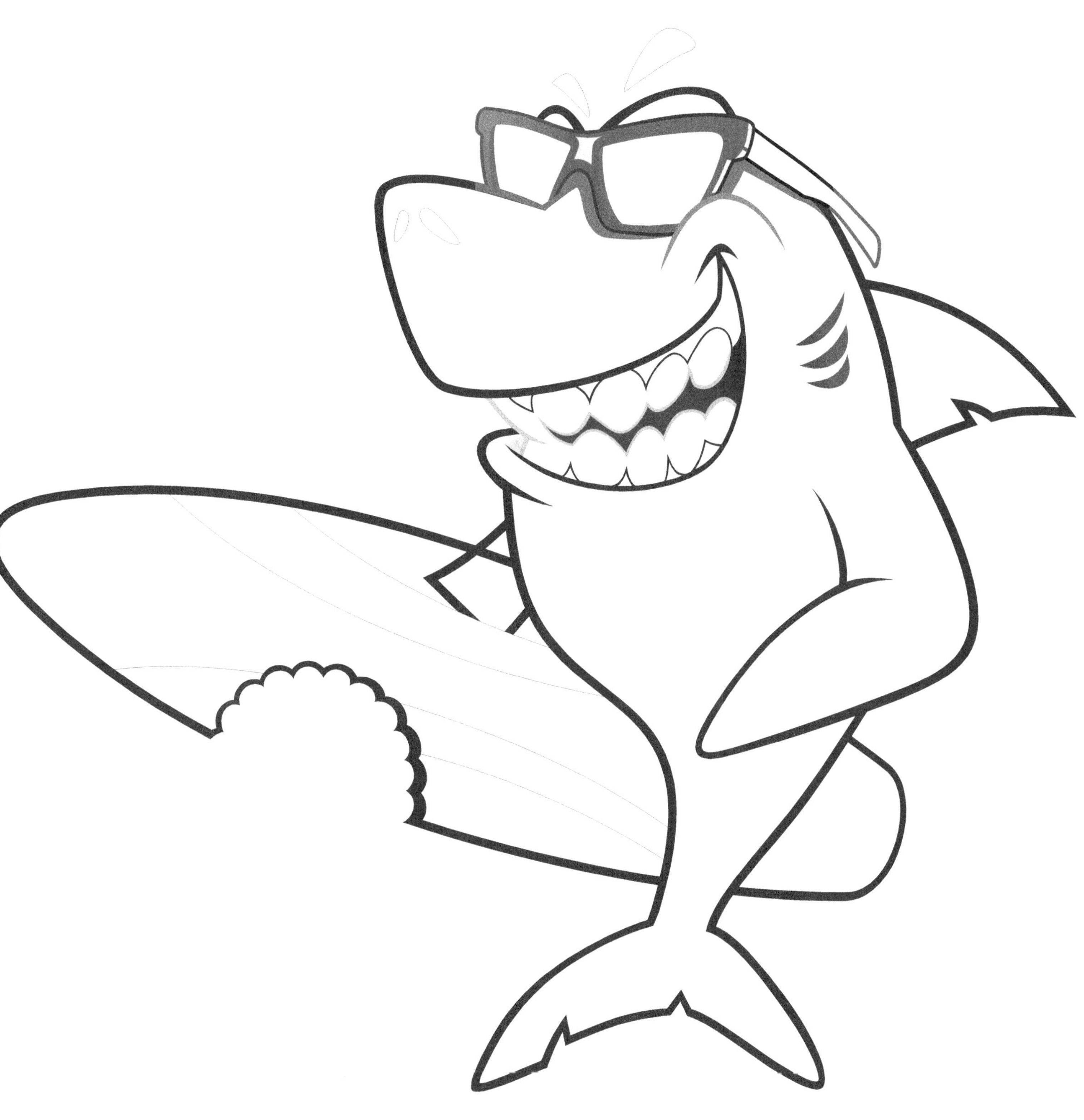